# GLUTEN FREE FEASTS

The Very Hungry Coeliac's
# GLUTEN FREE FEASTS

Gather and Share with
80 Sweet and Savoury Recipes

## Melanie Persson

photography by Ola O. Smit

*Hardie Grant*

BOOKS

# CONTENTS

6 Introduction
8 Kitchen Tools and Equipment
12 A Note on Ingredients
13 A Note on Other Allergens
14 Gluten-Free Flour 101
18 Basic Flour Blend
19 Dumpling Flour Blend

**21 Brunch Feast**
**51 Dim Sum Feast**
**87 Tea Party Feast**
**113 Picnic Feast**
**135 Game Day Feast**
**155 Taco Night Feast**
**171 Fish Shop Feast**
**189 Take Out Feast**
**211 Winter Warmer Feast**
**227 Celebration Feast**

249 Index
254 Acknowledgments
255 About the Author

# INTRODUCTION

My first book, *The Very Hungry Coeliac*, was wholeheartedly who I am as a cook. I had no idea how it would be received and whether I'd ever have the chance to write another. So naturally, I filled its pages with all my favourites – recipes that were very much borne from my personal experience and the food of my upbringing. In some ways, that's been freeing, because it allowed me to get that down on paper and then to move on, to grow as a cook and as a creator of gluten-free recipes. I see that book as a dedication to my own food journey, especially to the way I had to learn to adapt immediately after my coeliac diagnosis (which is why there's so much foundational information in there). Thankfully, this is something that resonated with many of you, for which I am so grateful.

This book, *Gluten Free Feasts*, I see as something a little different. I see it as a dedication to *you*, the person reading it, to either bring more food joy to your life, or to the life of a loved one. After all, as I was able to fulfil the cravings from my life pre-diagnosis, everything got so much easier. When those cravings were satisfied, I became happier to experiment and to learn a new way of cooking and living, which then drove more success with recipes and even more joy in food! It's like bringing back the love for cooking was step one, and I feel that was reflected in my first book. Now it's about moving beyond that, learning to live with coeliac disease and to live happily, which for me is so much about the sense of community that comes from making and sharing food. This book is therefore about the broader social aspects of being gluten free, about incorporating delicious gluten-free food into your life through family gatherings and events with friends. These are the aspects of living with coeliac disease or gluten intolerance that can be so hard to navigate.

The recipes in this book have been developed in collections, each aiming to fit within the scope of communal feasts and various opportunities for gathering around food. This is such a fundamental part of the human experience. It's *so* fundamental, in fact, that I think it's often taken for granted. That is, until it's no longer possible. Think about how often you catch up with your friends over a meal or plan the snacks you're going to need for a movie night or special occasion. Family gatherings so often centre around a meal, whether that's Sunday lunch or a picnic in the park. There really is a good reason that 'breaking bread' with someone is such a common phrase to reference connections made through food. And I think we don't speak enough about how this changes when someone has to make a medically necessary change to their diet – especially when it's as serious or debilitating as coeliac disease can be.

For those in the gluten-free community, every social event can present the potential for anxiety, sadness or disappointment, often underlying or even overshadowing the joy of celebrations and sharing. There can be anxiety about getting sick or being judged, sadness at having to bring your own food or from watching your gluten-free child be excluded, or disappointment from missing out on something everyone else is enjoying. I really want to help change that, by showing that it is very possible to incorporate gluten-free options into the food events that happen in our lives, great and small. This isn't always super simple – obviously, some things take more effort or energy than others. But I think you'll be surprised to find how easy it *can* be.

I've tried to include here everything I didn't have the time (or skill) for, when putting together my first book. This includes many staples from my day-to-day life, but also, lots of recipes requested by you! I thought it was important to ask you what was missing from your life, from my first book, from the gluten-free commercial food market more generally, and then try to fill those gaps. My ultimate goal is to feel that *nothing* is off-limits to us. I'm still working on that, but honestly, I really feel I've made leaps and bounds in the feasts included here. Throughout these pages, you'll find puff pastry, crumpets, steamed bao buns, croissants(!) and many other typically gluten-laden, hard-to-find foods. I'm so excited to share these recipes with you and I hope they can help to fill a gluten-shaped hole in your life or the lives of those around you. If there's one thing you take away from looking through these recipes, I hope it's that we can still 'break bread'. Let's just make it gluten free!

# KITCHEN TOOLS AND EQUIPMENT

Below are some of the tools I use frequently that I feel will really help to get you more comfortable in the kitchen. Obviously, wherever possible, I try to give you options and alternatives so that you don't *need* anything to make delicious food (the scales below are the exception!). However, as gluten-free cooking can be challenging enough at the best of times (not to mention a little more time-consuming as we often have to make more from scratch), I'm a huge fan of labour-saving hacks and tools. These things will not only make your life easier when cooking, but will also help to remove some margin for error or guesswork, which can be particularly helpful if you're not super confident in your kitchen yet.

## DIGITAL SCALES

I *highly* recommend you invest in a set of digital kitchen scales (these days, it's generally easy to find an affordable and reliable set). In fact, it's basically unavoidable for this book, but for very good reason. Cooking and baking are sciences, and this is even more true when working with gluten-free recipes as there are many more variables involved. Flour blends and individual starches do not all weigh the same, especially when factoring in inconsistent scooping, packing and levelling techniques. To get the most out of this book (not to mention cooking, more generally) weighing your ingredients will always give you the best, most consistent results. It will also make any potential troubleshooting a lot easier, as you will at least always know that the amounts and ratios you're working with are accurate, meaning you can rule this out as a potential issue and move onto any other problem areas.

As an added bonus, using digital scales means less mess and fewer dishes – there's no need to wash a whole set of measuring cups if you're adding the ingredients directly into a mixing bowl that is set on the scale. It's really a win-win!

**Note: All the recipes in the book were developed in gram and millilitre measurements, so I advise you to follow that set of measurements for the most accurate results. Most digital scales have a very simple function to switch between ounces and grams, so you can easily make the change. For accuracy, I do not advise using cup measurements, which is why they aren't included in this book.**

It may feel a bit finicky and strange at first, but I promise, you'll soon get the hang of what measuring in grams looks like for your ingredients, and everything will become so much faster. Then you'll be wondering how you ever cooked without scales in the first place!

## THERMOMETER

Where possible, I avoid the necessity of a thermometer by describing how you'll know something is at roughly the correct temperature. I'm talking about frying and caramelising here – obviously there's always a temperature given for baking, don't stress! Where I have done this, know that a precise temperature is not super important. There are a handful of recipes where I have included temperature ranges however, because I found that a little more specificity was required for optimal results. If those are recipes you plan to use frequently, I do suggest that an investment in a food thermometer may be a wise decision.

## PASTA MACHINE/ROLLER

My pasta roller may be my favourite labour-saving device in the kitchen. This is probably because my favourite foods are noodles and dumplings, and a pasta roller makes rolling dough so much faster. You might question that, thinking that dough for dumplings is generally rolled out one at a time, and you'd be right. That is the traditional method. However, I started using a pasta roller and a circular cookie cutter years ago to save myself time and I've never looked back. After all, as buying pre-made gluten-free wrappers isn't an option for us (yet, anyway), I figure we can use all the help we can get to speed up the process. You might be thinking, 'I'll never use a pasta roller because I don't eat dumplings or noodles,' but I use it to make fresh pasta as well, plus the phyllo pastry and lavosh crackers from my first book that can be rolled with a roller, too! Of course, all the foods I've mentioned can be made by hand, so it's not a deal-breaker, it's just a little gadget that I love. You can use a mechanical one or get an attachment for your stand mixer if you have one.

## FOOD PROCESSOR

A food processor is another very handy device to have in your kitchen. I use mine all the time to make food preparation that much faster. They're obviously great for chopping and mincing, but I also use mine to mix doughs. They're especially great for incorporating butter into flour when making pastry. You may be surprised that my go-to processor is actually an attachment for a stick blender (mine came in a set with two, different sized processing canisters), rather than a traditional counter-top appliance. I find this so much more portable, easy to store, and most importantly, easy to clean.

## STAND MIXER

I get asked about the necessity of a stand mixer for gluten-free cooking a lot and I think this comes from the misconception that gluten-free doughs do not need to be worked in the same way that gluten-filled doughs do. I understand where this comes from, after all, if there's no gluten to 'activate', why do we need to knead so thoroughly? The answer is that I find that the binders and starches used in gluten-free cooking actually do benefit significantly from thorough mixing. The texture of xanthan gum in particular changes noticeably from being mixed, becoming super sticky and elastic. This is essential to create gluten-free versions of typically gluten-filled foods. That's not to say that a stand mixer is essential, because doughs can be mixed by hand. But it can be difficult and time-consuming, as gluten-free dough is often wetter and stickier than you might expect. Kneading by hand on your work surface is therefore not ideal, and you'll need to mix doughs thoroughly with a wooden spoon or sturdy spatula instead. This is where the stand mixer comes in handy, as it can do this for you.

## OVEN AND OVEN THERMOMETER

The oven temperatures given in this book are for a fan oven, so convert where necessary for the oven in your kitchen. I have found that home kitchen ovens can be very temperamental, with hot spots or other inconsistencies. To prevent these from being an issue with your baking, an oven thermometer can be very useful. I have one that hangs from the central rack, and I'm able to check this as I'm cooking to make sure that the internal temperature of the oven is exactly what I've asked it to be!

# A NOTE ON INGREDIENTS

**It goes without saying that all ingredients used should be gluten free. Always check packets and labels to ensure that even traditionally non-gluten-containing items don't have 'may contain' warnings.**

### EGGS
The eggs I use throughout this book are all about 55g (2oz) without the shell. This is a medium egg in the UK, a large egg in the USA or Canada, and extra-large in Australia.

### MILK
I haven't specified the fat percentage of milk as it doesn't matter for these recipes. Simply use whichever you usually have to hand.

### BUTTER
Butter is always unsalted.

### GLUTEN-FREE CHICKEN POWDER
This is an Asian ingredient that's usually just called 'chicken powder' or sometimes 'chicken bouillon powder'. You'll be able to find it in your local Asian supermarket.

### GINGER
Ginger is always freshly grated root ginger, however you can use jarred ginger for ease. If doing so, I would recommend adding a little more than stated in the recipe to achieve the same intensity of flavour as using fresh.

### CITRUS
Always use unwaxed citrus when possible.

### GLUTEN-FREE GOCHUJANG PASTE
This is a fermented red chilli paste commonly used in Korean cooking. It can be tricky to find as many brands contain wheat or barley, but there are a few naturally gluten-free options and a couple of brands that are actually tested to be gluten free. Some large supermarkets stock it, otherwise there's generally a wide selection at Asian grocers for you to peruse.

### GLUTEN-FREE SOY SAUCE
Ensure all soy sauce used is gluten free. You should be able to find this in large supermarkets in the 'free-from' or 'world food' aisles.

### GLUTEN-FREE SHAOXING RICE WINE
You'll notice I use this a few times throughout the book. You need to ensure you use a gluten-free variety as it can sometimes contain yeasts derived from wheat. If you can't find gluten-free Shaoxing rice wine, you can use another sake or any other gluten-free rice wine. Pale dry sherry is also a good substitute.

### GLUTEN-FREE KEWPIE
This is a Japanese mayonnaise. It seems that the ingredients can change depending on where it's manufactured, so please always ensure you're using a gluten-free version. If you can't get hold of it, you can simply use regular gluten-free mayonnaise.

### GLUTEN-FREE BAKING POWDER AND CORNFLOUR (CORNSTARCH)
These should always be gluten free but please be sure to check the label of the product you are buying to ensure it doesn't contain any products derived from wheat.

# A NOTE ON OTHER ALLERGENS

When I create recipes, I'm aiming for the best possible version I can achieve to mimic the flavour and texture of the 'normal', gluten-filled iteration. While I always have other allergens in mind, achieving the ultimate gluten-free recipe is the goal, and it's not always possible to do that *and* remove dairy, eggs or other allergens. For some recipes, swaps will not matter in the slightest, but for some more finicky recipes, there is generally a very good reason I opt to include eggs or dairy products (as a protein source, for instance, to assist in the binding properties of certain doughs). Unfortunately, it's just not possible for one person (me!) to rule out each specific allergen for each recipe, without compromising on quality. This means that, sometimes, some experimentation on your part will be required. My hope is that through teaching you the *why* behind my recipes and the science of gluten-free cooking, you'll be better equipped to tackle these issues if they arise. When you're really stumped, I am usually very on top of my messages on social media platforms and when I have time, I'm happy to help point you in the right direction!

On a separate but related note, I'll repeat what I said at the beginning of my first book: this is not a 'health-focused' recipe book. There are ample gluten-free cookbooks that aim to cut out or reduce sugar, carbohydrates and starches, as well as other allergens. There is absolutely a place for those books – I'm grateful to them because they taught me a lot in the early stages of my gluten-free cooking journey. This book, however, is not one of them. My work is about unapologetically delicious food, which is about indulgence and luxury as much as it is about flavour and abundance. After all,

I don't think being gluten-free should mean we are excluded from the indulgences 'regular' people enjoy once in a while. You can, of course, tweak where you see fit, but bear in mind that where you see sources of sweetness, there is a good reason for its inclusion (sugar in bread, for example, is there because yeast requires sugar to rise and therefore helps to create light, fluffy-textured doughs). Similarly, the use of starches in recipes rather than high-protein flours is also what makes these recipes mimic their gluten-laden counterparts, without denseness or gummy textures. Please do not try to substitute something like rice flour with brown rice flour, or sorghum for tapioca, for instance, as the absorbency rates are vastly different and will alter the recipe and final product dramatically!

# GLUTEN-FREE FLOUR 101

**One of the most important things to understand when you start cooking or baking gluten free is that there is no one-for-one substitute for wheat flour. Any gluten-free flour you see labelled as gluten-free 'plain flour', 'self-raising flour', or 'all-purpose flour' and so on, is actually a *blend* of various flours or starches that is designed to mimic the properties of wheat flour. That is simple enough to understand, but in practice, this is where a lot of people struggle.**

The reality is that all these blends vary, being made up of different ratios of starches, flours and thickeners or binders that all behave slightly differently. This means that you can follow a gluten-free recipe to a tee, but if you use a different flour to the one used by the recipe creator, this can be enough to change the results of the recipe.

Similarly, if you follow a regular, gluten-filled recipe and attempt to substitute a gluten-free flour blend for the wheat flour, you may not achieve the desired results. This varies a lot, because after all, different food products call for gluten to act in different ways, and there are even variations among wheat flours to accommodate these. Think of 'cake flour' that is typically low in gluten so that cakes can be light and airy, or 'bread flour' that has a higher gluten content for nicely textured loaves. Creating a gluten-free flour is therefore as much about understanding the role of gluten in regular foods as it is about understanding various gluten-free ingredients. You need to consider what gluten is doing in any given food in order to figure out how these properties can be mimicked to replace the flavour and texture in a gluten-free version. In short, creating a universal flour blend that is going to be as versatile as wheat flour (when wheat flour itself isn't a one-size-fits-all) is simply impossible. Or at least, it is at the moment, with the food science and technology at hand (I'm still crossing my fingers that this will be invented some day!).

If you have some experience cooking or baking with gluten-free flours, you may have found that some things can be converted more easily than others. Generally speaking, things like cakes or brownies, for instance, are quite forgiving, as these are foods that don't rely heavily on gluten for texture. It can be a dramatically different experience trying to make something like bread, pasta, noodles or dumpling wrappers. If you've tried to make these with a basic supermarket blend in the past, it's very likely you ended up with a dense or crumbly mess. That is because these are foods that typically depend heavily on gluten to create a dough that can be stretched, rolled thin and shaped, all while maintaining their structural integrity. Of course, I demonstrate through my recipes that these things are very possible to make gluten free, but they do require some extra ingredients that are generally not found in a typical supermarket flour blend.

## MY BASIC FLOUR BLEND

I'm giving you all this information about gluten-free flours so that you can understand why I created the blend that I use throughout this book (page 18). I want to be sure that you can achieve the same results as me, without being limited by the availability of a specific commercial flour. I also hope that by seeing how I tweak my base blend in certain recipes (by adding various other components), I can show how individual ingredients work and how they can be customised to work for whatever you are trying to make.

I am well aware that this can be intimidating or frustrating, especially if you're new to the world of gluten-free cooking. I'm sorry, I've been there, and I get it. But please know that this really is in the name of making the best possible food, with the most consistent results. And you won't mind the initial effort expended to make the flour blend when you start cooking and eating food you haven't been able to enjoy in a long time!

My **basic flour blend** (page 18) is used in most of the recipes in this book (and my first book, too) and should therefore be the first thing you make as it cannot simply be substituted for any old gluten-free plain (all-purpose) flour stocked in a supermarket. You'll see it (and my **dumpling flour blend**; page 19) highlighted in **bold** in the ingredients lists of the recipes that use it. I make it in 1–2 kg (2¼–4½ lb) batches and keep it handy in my pantry. I do find it to be very versatile for my cooking in general, beyond the recipes in this book. However, as I can't test it with every recipe that exists, I can't guarantee it will always produce perfect results. I have heard from many readers of my first book that it has become their go-to basic flour of choice, which is fantastic!

## IMPORTANT NOTES

It is very important that you start off on the right foot where the flour blend is concerned. I get asked quite a lot if you can substitute other flours for any of the base ingredients – typically whether brown rice flour can be used instead of white. The simple answer is NO. To work around allergens, there are some options (see overleaf), but I absolutely do not recommend substituting a whole grain flour for any of the starches in the blend, nor can you introduce an entirely different flour. Unfortunately, they are simply not interchangeable, usually because of the drastically different rates of water absorbency that will heavily affect the ratios in each and every recipe.

There are also some variations among flours that you should watch out for when gathering the ingredients for the flour blend. Note that each starch in the blend should be the white (or very slightly off-white), finely ground variety that feels powdery to the touch, like icing (powdered) sugar. There are some products marketed as 'rice flour' that are quite coarse (this is what is used in some traditional shortbread recipes). Avoid these, and same goes for various cornflours (cornstarch) as well. The cornflour needed for my basic flour blend is the white, powdery starch often used for thickening. This is as opposed to the various cornflours used in Latin American cooking, for instance, that are milled and processed to a coarser consistency for tortillas, arepas and other corn-based foods. The best place to purchase rice, tapioca and potato starches, if they're not available in major supermarkets, is generally an Asian grocer (local shops or online). They're usually also the most cost-effective choice.

It is also essential to understand that this blend is exactly as it sounds – a basic flour blend. It is designed as a substitute for a standard gluten-free plain (all-purpose) flour, not a bread flour or pasta flour, or any other specialty flour that you can sometimes find commercially. This means that it will not work well on its own for things like bread or pasta. As I've explained above, things that rely heavily on gluten require some additional ingredients, and these are added in each recipe as necessary. The main point of difference in these recipes is psyllium husk powder.

## PSYLLIUM HUSK

Psyllium husk has become a relatively well-known ingredient in gluten-free cooking over the past few years, thanks largely to its usefulness in the production of gluten-free bread. I generally see the whole husks mixed with water to create a gel, which is then added to flour to help form a workable dough. I prefer not to do this, as I don't love the texture it creates in the finished bread product. I've also found that it's completely unnecessary when the husk can be milled into a powder and added to other dry ingredients. This makes it basically invisible in the finished product and means it can also be added to thinner, silkier doughs, without marring the texture with the large husk granules. I do this with egg noodles (page 202) and croissants (page 38), for example, as well as the pasta and phyllo pastry that are in my first book.

My preferred method of using psyllium husk is to purchase the husks whole (from supermarkets, health food stores or online), and then to blitz them myself (any blender or high-powered food processor should do the trick). You can buy psyllium husk powder, but this is often a slightly different variety to the husks that are generally sold whole, and may alter the colour of your baked goods. This doesn't affect the flavour though, so if the ready powdered form is all that is available to you, don't worry.

## WORKING AROUND ALLERGENS

If you've read through the information on gluten-free flours and flour blends, you'll understand why it is not super easy to just switch out or remove any one of the starches that make up the base blend. This is a blend that has been developed over many years to be as versatile as possible and, most importantly, it's also been used to develop the recipes in this book. If you have an allergy to one of the individual starches, I'd recommend removing it, and scaling the quantity of the other starches to maintain the ratio of starch to xanthan gum in the initial mix. For a corn allergy for instance, removing the 250 g (9 oz) of cornflour (cornstarch) would mean increasing the amount of rice flour to 423 g (15¼ oz), the tapioca to 336 g (11⅚ oz), and the potato starch to 221 g (7¾ oz). You can round these to the nearest 5 g (¼ oz), I've just included the precise amounts so you can see how I've altered them but maintained the proportions in the original blend. I can't guarantee that this will work flawlessly in each and every recipe, but that is the best way to go about working around an allergy to a specific starch in the base blend.

# BASIC FLOUR BLEND

This is the plain (all-purpose) flour blend I've created to be used in most of the recipes in this book. To convert this flour into a self-raising blend, simply add 1 teaspoon of gluten-free baking powder for every 100 g (3½ oz) of this mix (this is best added as needed on the day of baking).

Note that all starches used in this blend should be the super finely ground variety (see Important Notes on page 15 for more details). This recipe was developed in gram measurements, so I advise you to follow that set of measurements for the most accurate results.

Sift the ingredients into a large bowl and mix until well combined. Sift and mix again to ensure the starches and xanthan gum have been evenly distributed into a homogenous flour blend. Store in an airtight container until ready to use.

| Makes 1 kg (2¼ lb) | Makes 2 kg (4½ lb) |
| --- | --- |
| 315 g (11¼ oz) rice flour | 630 g (22¼ oz) rice flour |
| 250 g (9 oz) tapioca starch | 500 g (17¾ oz) tapioca starch |
| 250 g (9 oz) gluten-free cornflour (cornstarch) | 500 g (17¾ oz) gluten-free cornflour (cornstarch) |
| 165 g (5¾ oz) potato starch | 330 g (11½ oz) potato starch |
| 2 tablespoons + 1 teaspoon xanthan gum | 40 g (1½ oz) xanthan gum |

# DUMPLING FLOUR BLEND

This is the blend I created specifically for dumplings. I use it for all the dumpling wrappers in this book (pages 52 and 57). As with the basic flour blend, all starches used in this are the super finely ground variety. Again, I've included recipes scaled for 1 kg (2¼ lb) and 2 kg (4½ lb) batches, as having this ready in your pantry is a real time-saver when you need a dumpling fix!

Note that sweet potato starch can be a little tricky to track down. It can also be confusing because some brands use the labels of sweet potato 'starch', 'powder' or 'flour' interchangeably, while others differentiate 'starch' (which always refers to the powdery white type) from the coarser 'flour' (which is darker in colour). The latter will not work properly, so be sure to find and use the white, starchy flour. Asian supermarkets are the place to look for it (try online if your local doesn't stock it). If you struggle to find it, you can use regular potato starch. It's not quite as perfect but still works very well. This recipe was developed in gram measurements, so I advise you to follow that set of measurements for the most accurate results.

Sift the ingredients into a large bowl and mix until well combined. Sift and mix again to ensure the starches and xanthan gum have been evenly distributed into a homogenous flour blend. Store in an airtight container until ready to use.

| Makes 1 kg (2¼ lb) | Makes 2 kg (4½ lb) |
| --- | --- |
| 300 g (10½ oz) glutinous rice flour | 600 g (21 oz) glutinous rice flour |
| 295 g (10½ oz) tapioca starch | 590 g (20¾ oz) tapioca starch |
| 185 g (6½ oz) rice flour | 370 g (13 oz) rice flour |
| 185 g (6½ oz) sweet potato starch | 370 g (13 oz) sweet potato starch |
| 35 g (1¼ oz) xanthan gum | 70 g (2½ oz) xanthan gum |

# BRUNCH FEAST

I think brunch is my favourite meal of the day, largely because I love that anything goes. Whether it's delicate pastries, nibbles, or full savoury meals, you're guaranteed a good time, especially when this is accompanied by a lovely coffee. In this feast, I've included my favourite brunch staples with a focus on things that are generally hard to find gluten-free versions of, including (most excitingly) croissants, as well as waffles, hot cross buns, crumpets, and more. Whatever you're in the mood for, you're bound to find something delectable you want to indulge in on the weekend.

# FLUFFY PANCAKES WITH MASCARPONE + BLUEBERRY COMPOTE

Makes 6–8

**Breakfast classic. 'Nuff said. Enjoy!**

60 g (2 oz) **basic flour blend** (page 18)
120 g (4¼ oz) rice flour
2 teaspoons gluten-free baking powder
40 g (1½ oz) caster (superfine) sugar
⅛ teaspoon salt
2 eggs
2 teaspoons vanilla bean paste (or extract)
250 ml (8½ fl oz) milk
20 g (¾ oz) unsalted butter, melted
2–3 teaspoons vegetable oil, for frying

Sift the dry ingredients into a large bowl, then create a well in the centre and add the eggs, vanilla and half the milk. Whisk gently, incorporating the dry ingredients from the side of the bowl to create a thick batter. When smooth, whisk in the remaining milk. Adding the milk in batches helps to prevent lumps forming in the batter. Add the melted butter and stir again, then set aside for 15 minutes.

Place a large non-stick frying pan over medium heat and grease with a little of the oil to lightly coat the frying pan; wipe away the excess with paper towel. When hot, use a ladle or measuring cup to pour the batter into the pan (75 ml/ 2½ fl oz of batter makes a nice size pancake).

When lots of bubbles start to appear and pop on the top of the pancake, flip it over using a spatula and cook the reverse side for a further 2–3 minutes. Transfer to a preheated oven (set to about 60°C Fan/140°F Fan) to keep warm. Repeat with the remaining batter, greasing the pan with more oil between each pancake. Transfer to a plate and serve while hot with the vanilla mascarpone and blueberry compote.

## VANILLA MASCARPONE

250 g (9 oz) mascarpone
2 teaspoons honey (or to taste)
1 teaspoon vanilla bean paste (or extract)
⅛ teaspoon salt

Combine all the ingredients in a small bowl and mix well. Adjust the ratio of honey and salt slightly according to taste. Dollop onto freshly cooked pancakes along with a fruit compote or jam (jelly).

## BLUEBERRY COMPOTE

200 g (7 oz) frozen blueberries
1 teaspoon lemon juice
1 tablespoon caster (superfine) sugar (or to taste)

Place half the blueberries in a small saucepan with the lemon juice and sugar and set over medium heat. Stir occasionally, for 5–10 minutes, while the berries thaw and start to break down. Allow to simmer and reduce slightly, then add the remaining berries and cook for 3–4 minutes more until they're heated through and starting to soften.

Remove from the heat and transfer to a serving bowl, then spoon onto pancakes to serve.

# CRUMPETS

### Makes about 6

I'm so excited to share these with you as crumpets are a recipe I've been developing for a long time. Ensure you allow enough time for the batter to prove (as this is a yeast-based recipe) and, although it will be tempting to try these immediately after the first cook, resist! Follow the cooling and toasting instructions carefully for the very best results.

250 ml (8½ fl oz) warm milk (37–40°C/100–105°F is ideal)
1½ teaspoons instant dried yeast
4 teaspoons caster (superfine) sugar
60 g (2 oz) **basic flour blend** (page 18)
120 g (4¼ oz/scant 1 cup) rice flour
¼ teaspoon salt
½ teaspoon psyllium husk powder
1 teaspoon gluten-free baking powder
2 eggs
20 g (¾ oz) unsalted butter, melted, plus extra for greasing
2–3 teaspoons vegetable oil, for frying

Add the milk to a medium jug (pitcher) or bowl, then mix in the yeast and 2 teaspoons of the sugar. Cover and leave in a warm, draft-free place for 10 minutes until the yeast has 'bloomed', which means there is a thick layer of foam on the surface. (If a layer of foam has not formed, your yeast may not be active and the crumpets will not work properly. See page 36 for guidance on working with yeast.)

Meanwhile, in a large mixing bowl, whisk together the remaining dry ingredients, including the remaining 2 teaspoons of sugar. Create a well in the centre.

Whisk the eggs into the milk-yeast mixture, then pour this into the dry ingredients along with the melted butter. Whisk well to form a smooth batter, then cover the bowl first with cling film (plastic wrap), then with a tea towel (dish towel), and leave to prove in a warm, draft-free place for 45 minutes.

Place a large, non-stick frying pan over low heat and grease with a little vegetable oil. Allow the pan to heat up while you grease your crumpet rings generously with extra butter. Place as many rings as will fit in the pan, then add about 75 ml (2½ fl oz) of the crumpet batter to each ring.

Cook for 5–6 minutes until the crumpets have set around the edges and bubbles have appeared all over the surface. The base of the crumpets should be a deep, golden brown. Remove the crumpet rings, then flip the crumpets and cook for a further 2–3 minutes. Transfer to a cooling rack to cool completely.

Do not be tempted to serve the crumpets immediately as the internal crumb needs to cool and set first. Once completely cool, toast the crumpets in a dry frying pan or toaster until crisp on both sides, then serve immediately. Untoasted, these will keep in an airtight container for 2–3 days (they also freeze well).

NOTE

*Of course, you'll need a few crumpet rings to make these, but it's well worth it to enjoy these airy little morsels slathered in butter, honey, or whatever you prefer!*

# HOT CROSS BUNS

*Makes 9*

Hot cross buns are generally reserved for the months around Easter, but I'd argue that because gluten-free people tend to miss out a lot, we have a lot of catching up to do. These are delightfully soft and squishy; with all the sweetness and spices I remember from the hot cross buns of my childhood. I'm sure you're going to love them.

220 ml (7½ fl oz) warm water (37–40°C/100–105°F is ideal)
1 tablespoon instant dried yeast
90 g (3 oz) soft light brown sugar
280 g (10 oz) **basic flour blend** (page 18), plus extra for dusting
1 tablespoon psyllium husk powder
1 teaspoon xanthan gum
1 teaspoon gluten-free baking powder
½ teaspoon salt
2 teaspoons ground cinnamon
1 teaspoon ground nutmeg
½ teaspoon ground allspice
¼ teaspoon ground ginger
100 g (3½ oz) mixed dried fruit
2 eggs
1 teaspoon vanilla bean paste (or extract)
40 g (1½ oz) unsalted butter, chilled and cubed, plus extra for glazing
vegetable oil, for greasing

**For the egg wash**
1 egg yolk
2 tablespoons single (light) cream

**For the crosses**
35 g (1¼ oz) **basic flour blend** (page 18)
45 ml (1½ fl oz) water (at room temperature)

Add the warm water to a medium jug (pitcher) or bowl, then mix in the yeast and 30 g (1 oz) of the sugar. Cover and leave in a warm, draft-free place for 10 minutes until the yeast has 'bloomed', which means there is a thick layer of foam on the surface. (If a layer of foam has not formed, your yeast may not be active and the buns will not work properly. See page 36 for guidance on working with yeast.)

Meanwhile, combine the flour, psyllium husk powder, xanthan gum, baking powder, salt, spices and the remaining 60 g (2 oz) sugar in the bowl of a stand mixer.

In a separate bowl, dust the mixed dried fruit with 2 teaspoons of extra flour, then set aside.

Whisk the eggs and vanilla into the water-yeast mixture, then pour this into the dry ingredients. Mix slowly (with the paddle attachment) until mostly combined, then mix vigorously (medium speed on a mixer) for 4–5 minutes, scraping down the side of the bowl once or twice to ensure all the ingredients are combining.

When the dough is smooth (it will still be quite wet and sticky), add the cubed butter, then run the mixer until no lumps of butter remain.

Grease a large bowl with vegetable oil, then transfer and gather the dough into it. Shake and rotate the bowl a little to ensure the dough is a uniform ball, then flip it over. The aim is to have a smooth ball of dough that is greased all over, not to incorporate more fat into the dough, so try to avoid handling it and dimpling the dough with your fingers. Cover the bowl first with cling film (plastic wrap), then with a tea towel (dish towel) and place it in a warm, draft-free place for 1 hour.

...continues overleaf

While the dough is proving, grease a 16 × 25 cm (6¼ × 9¾ in) baking dish with vegetable oil.

Lightly dust a large work surface with extra flour. Tip out the proved dough onto the surface and lightly dust the dough with flour, too. Knead the dough by hand for 30–40 seconds, removing the air bubbles until it is smooth, dusting lightly with more flour only as absolutely necessary to prevent it sticking.

Divide the dough into 9 equal portions. Use your hands to roll these into smooth balls, then arrange them evenly in the greased baking dish. Cover the dish first with cling film (plastic wrap), then with a tea towel (dish towel), and leave to prove in a warm, draft-free place for 45–60 minutes, or until the buns have grown in size by about 50%.

Towards the end of the proving time, preheat the oven to 160°C Fan (325°F Fan).

Prepare the egg wash by beating together the egg yolk and cream in a small bowl.

Prepare the mixture for the crosses by combining the flour and water until smooth, then transfer it to a piping or sandwich bag.

When the buns have proved, gently brush the tops of the buns with a light layer of egg wash, then cut a small hole in the bag with the cross mixture and pipe the cross design onto the buns.

Transfer the buns to the preheated oven and bake for 26–28 minutes, or until golden brown.

When cooked, remove the buns from the oven and glaze them by running a little cold butter all over the tops (this is optional but softens the crust and adds extra flavour and shine). Allow the buns to cool in the baking dish for at least 30 minutes before serving.

NOTE

*You can do most of the work for these the day before you want to eat them, then simply prove them overnight, so that you have delicious, freshly baked hot cross buns for brunch in the morning. To do this, follow the recipe as instructed for the first prove and the shaping of the buns. Then, instead of proving the buns for 40–60 minutes in a warm environment, cover and refrigerate the buns for 8–12 hours. In the morning, remove them from the fridge and leave them in a warm place for 90 minutes, or until doubled in size, then bake.*

# CRISPY WAFFLES

### Makes about 4

These have been a staple in my house with family and friends for years and, although none of them need to eat gluten free, they still request these on repeat. They're crispy on the outside and fluffy on the inside. I love eating them with butterscotch sauce, and often ice cream, too (both overleaf). They're also a fantastic base for savoury options like bacon or fried chicken.

60 g (2 oz) **basic flour blend** (page 18)
110 g (4 oz) rice flour
45 g (1¼ oz) tapioca starch
¼ teaspoon salt
2 tablespoon caster (superfine) sugar
2½ teaspoons gluten-free baking powder
2 eggs
1½ teaspoons vanilla bean paste (or extract)
280 ml (9½ fl oz) milk
40 g (1½ oz) unsalted butter, melted

Sift the dry ingredients into a large bowl, then create a well in the centre and add the eggs and vanilla. Pour in half the milk and mix well until a thick, smooth batter has formed, then whisk in the remaining milk. Add the melted butter to the batter and mix to combine, then cover and set the batter aside for 10 minutes.

Meanwhile, preheat your waffle iron to the highest heat setting.

Now cook your waffles. The amount of batter you need to add to your iron will depend on its size, so this may take a little trial and error. The waffles cook best when the waffle iron is full, as this ensures full contact of the batter to the heated plates. Mine takes 130–160 ml (4½–5½ fl oz) of batter per waffle. The cooking time and temperature will also vary by brand. I find that cooking at a high heat for 3–4 minutes is best, giving you a deep golden brown, crispy exterior and a fluffy middle.

Remove the cooked waffles from the iron with two skewers, held like prongs (push them into the sides of the waffle, then lift the waffle out of the iron). Transfer the cooked waffles to a cooling rack and remove the skewers. The skewering also creates two holes that allow excess steam to escape from the waffle; in combination with the air circulating around the cooling rack, this should keep them crisp.

Allow the waffles to cool for 1–2 minutes before plating and serving with butterscotch sauce (overleaf) or your favourite toppings. If not serving straight away, transfer to a rack in a preheated oven (set to about 60°C Fan/140°F Fan) to keep them hot and crisp until ready to serve. Alternatively, let them cool completely before storing in an airtight container for 2–3 days (they also freeze well). Reheat in a toaster until crisp or in the oven at around 180°C Fan (350°F Fan) for 8–10 minutes (15–20 minutes if cooking from frozen).

NOTE

*These obviously require a waffle iron to make. My recipe is best suited to thicker waffles styles that are square or round and 2–3 cm (about 1 in) thick at the thickest point, rather than clover-shaped waffles that are about 1 cm (½ in) thick. You can still use this batter to make thin waffles; they will just be crispier (and I think contrast between a crisp exterior and fluffy interior is what makes these special!).*

pictured overleaf

# NO-CHURN WHISKEY BUTTERSCOTCH ICE-CREAM

Serves 6

This is an incredibly decadent accompaniment for brunch, but I've included it because of how easy it is to make and how delicious it is on waffles (page 27), especially with extra lashings of butterscotch sauce (below). The whiskey might seem a little cheeky, but I promise it's well worth it, not just for the delicious flavour, but because this is the secret to achieving a no-churn ice cream that remains light and creamy, even when fully frozen. As alcoholic liquors don't freeze, adding whiskey to a simple cream base prevents it from freezing solid, which is generally the major downfall of no-churn ice cream recipes. I recommend following the recipe as written with the three tablespoons of whiskey – this yields a softer, more scoopable ice cream with a delicious whiskey flavour – however, you can reduce the whiskey to a single tablespoon if you'd prefer little-to-no whiskey flavour and a firmer ice cream texture.

400 ml (14 fl oz) whipping cream
200 g (7 oz) sweetened condensed milk
3 tablespoons whiskey
2 teaspoons vanilla bean paste (or extract)
pinch of salt
4–5 tablespoons **butterscotch sauce** (below)

In a large mixing bowl or the bowl of a stand mixer, add all the ingredients except the butterscotch sauce. Using an electric hand mixer or the stand mixer, whisk on medium speed until medium-stiff peaks form.

Transfer one-third of the mixture to a large airtight container, spread it into an even layer with a spatula, then drizzle over 1–2 tablespoons of butterscotch sauce. Repeat with two more layers, then seal the container and transfer to the freezer.

Freeze for 4–5 hours or overnight before serving.

## BUTTERSCOTCH SAUCE

Makes about 250 g (9 oz)

100 g (3½ oz) unsalted butter
100 g (3½ oz) soft light brown sugar
60 g (2¼ oz) single (light) cream
¼ teaspoon salt

Place the butter and sugar in a small saucepan set over medium heat. Allow the butter to melt and the sugar to dissolve, stirring gently with a spatula. When fully combined, add the cream and salt and stir again to incorporate the cream and dissolve the salt.

Transfer to a pouring jug and serve warm or, if storing, allow to cool completely before transferring to a sealed container or jar in the fridge for a few days. Reheat gently in a saucepan before serving.

# 'BAKED' BEANS

Serves 4–6

These aren't actually baked, but then I'm not sure whether most beans served in cafés are these days, anyway? Either way, they're rich, smoky, and packed with flavour – perfect for a big brunch at home served with my potato & carrot röstis (opposite).

2 tablespoon extra virgin olive oil
2 onions, diced
2 red (bell) peppers, deseeded and sliced
¾ teaspoon salt, plus extra to taste
3 garlic cloves, minced
1–2 tablespoons harissa paste
1 teaspoon smoked paprika
1 teaspoon ground coriander
½ teaspoon ground cumin
¼ teaspoon cracked black pepper
1 teaspoon dried oregano
½ teaspoon dried parsley
¾ teaspoon caster (superfine) sugar
500 ml (17 fl oz) tomato passata
2 × 400 g (14 oz) cans cannellini beans, drained and rinsed

Heat a large frying pan over medium heat and add the oil, onions, red peppers and salt. Cook until the vegetables are tender and the onion is translucent, then add the garlic. Cook for 1–2 minutes until fragrant, then add all the remaining ingredients except for the tomato passata and cannellini beans.

Mix everything until well combined, then stir in the tomato passata and beans. Bring to a simmer and allow to cook for 10–15 minutes until the tomato sauce has reduced by about a quarter, stirring frequently.

Season with a little extra salt to taste, then remove from the heat and serve with good quality toasted gluten-free bread and eggs cooked your preferred way!

NOTE

*Harissa pastes vary quite a lot in intensity, so I've indicated using 1–2 tablespoons so you can adjust to taste.*

*If you have any leftovers, you can add more tomato passata and a little more salt and pepper (I sometimes fry off some chorizo and add that as well), then use it as a base for a shakshuka-style breakfast (where eggs are cooked in a spiced tomato sauce). This is a great way to make one meal stretch to two!*

pictured overleaf

# POTATO + CARROT RÖSTIS

Makes about 6

I worked as a nanny on and off throughout university and this is something I actually used to make for the kids. The wonderful parents I worked with were busy and worked long hours, so sometimes by the end of the week there wouldn't be a lot of groceries left and I'd have to get creative based on what I could find in the pantry. There were always plenty of veggies, but one night, that proved to be a particularly hard sell. I ended up tempting the kids with the idea of hashbrowns instead and made these. They went down an absolute treat and since then have become a regular in my brunch rotation. I like to use them as a substitute for toast with eggs and hollandaise, or as part of a big brekkie, with bacon, mushrooms and all the sides!

2–3 medium potatoes, peeled (about 400–500 g/ 14–18 oz)
1 carrot, peeled
2–3 spring onions (scallions), finely sliced
½ teaspoon garlic powder
½ teaspoon salt
½ teaspoon cracked black pepper (or to taste)
2–3 tablespoons vegetable oil, for frying
1 teaspoon unsalted butter, for frying

Place a large, clean tea towel (dish towel) on top of a chopping board and grate (shred) the potatoes and carrot directly onto it. Gather the corners of the tea towel, collecting the vegetables in the middle, and squeeze over the sink to extract as much excess liquid as possible.

Transfer the grated vegetables to a bowl along with the spring onions, garlic powder, salt and pepper, then toss everything together with your hands.

Heat a large frying pan (skillet) over low-medium heat, then add enough vegetable oil to generously coat the surface. Add the butter too and swirl the pan to melt and mix it with the oil.

Working in batches, place large spoonfuls of the vegetable mixture into the pan, with space between each, then use the spoon to shape them into rough patties about 10 cm (4 in) wide. Don't compress the patties as this will make them dense and soggy. Allow to cook for 8–9 minutes, touching them as little as possible, until the bases are golden brown. Flip and cook for a further 6–8 minutes, adding a little more oil if needed. Once crisp and cooked through, transfer to a plate lined with paper towel while you cook the rest. Serve hot with your favourite eggs.

NOTE

*I make individual röstis, but you can use the total mixture to make one giant rösti instead. If doing so, you may have to increase the cooking time a little.*

pictured overleaf

# CROISSANTS: AN INTRODUCTION

Makes 6–8

I'm not sure I ever really entertained the idea that gluten-free croissants were a possibility. Over the years, I tried many versions from bakeries, attempted various recipes I found online, and eventually started experimenting myself when none of them hit the spot.
I never had much success until I got onto the early stages of this recipe. The first results absolutely blew me away so, naturally, I started working to perfect it immediately, and I'm so happy with the final product! I even shed a few tears when I sliced into the first successful croissant (and then again when I actually tasted it). These pastries are buttery and light; crisp and flaky on the outside and tender on the inside. The dough holds the layers of butter and stretches around them beautifully in the oven, so that you end up with the open, honeycomb texture characteristic of a good croissant. I've seriously never had anything like it since being gluten free. Even my gluten-eating friends enjoy them!

I'll say upfront that this is likely not a recipe for beginner bakers. I wouldn't say that it's exclusively for advanced bakers, but it definitely takes a little determination, and prior baking experience will absolutely help. After all, even gluten-filled croissants are a notorious pressure point for bakers so, of course, the gluten-free version isn't going to be easier. Saying that, I've really tried to keep things as simple as possible and provided extra explanation where I think it's needed. Please read through this guide before starting – I really want you to be armed with as much knowledge as possible before you take them on!

## AN OVERVIEW

The first thing to be aware of is that these need to be made over two days. Please understand that I don't make these rules, this is very standard – in fact, some bakers of regular croissants make them over three days!

### Day One
30–60 minutes of prep the evening before you want to bake them.

### Day Two
1–2 hours of hands-on preparation.
3–4 hours of proving, cooking and cooling.

This recipe makes either 6 small–medium croissants or 3 medium–large ones. I know this is quite a small quantity for such a labour of love but, unfortunately, increasing the amount of dough makes the process significantly more challenging, not only in working with the dough but in maintaining the crucial butter layers. I've prioritised helping you to make the best croissant possible, rather than a larger number of imperfect croissants.

If you happen to have access to a dough sheeter (a piece of commercial bakery equipment that will roll the dough for you) it would be possible to double or triple the recipe. However, bear in mind that the measurements provided for the butter sheets, and for cutting and folding the dough, would not be applicable.

### MIXING THE DOUGH

The dough comes together relatively easily, but it does need to be mixed very thoroughly and it is too wet and sticky to be kneaded by hand. The easiest way is to use a stand mixer fitted with a paddle beater (it takes 8–10 minutes this way), but you can use a sturdy spatula or wooden spoon, too. If doing things by hand though, it might pay to enlist some help as it takes a fair bit of elbow grease and vigorous mixing for 10–15 minutes. You might question why such thorough mixing is needed when there is no gluten to 'activate'. Essentially, the binders we're using to mimic the effects of gluten (psyllium husk, xanthan gum and egg) work best, and provide the most elasticity and structural integrity, when kneaded, mixed or blitzed thoroughly (I discuss binders in more detail in my first book, *The Very Hungry Coeliac*).

### CHILLING THE DOUGH

The dough undergoes the first prove overnight in the fridge. This helps with the texture of the dough, giving it time to hydrate to the right consistency and therefore makes it easier to roll out. It also helps to develop flavour. Note that during the lamination process (creating the layers of butter within the dough), I don't chill as consistently or for as long as 'normal' croissant recipes recommend. This is because chilling for too long once the butter is enclosed in the dough can make it a little too brittle. It should, however, be cool to the touch. If you're making these in a warm kitchen and/or in summertime, you will likely need to work quickly and refrigerate the dough a few times as you work through the lamination process.

### UNDERSTANDING THE 'BUTTER SHEET' METHOD

My method for laminating butter into this dough is a little unorthodox. Typically, a single slab of butter is placed in the centre of a rolled sheet of dough, and the dough is folded around to enclose it. The dough is then rolled and folded several times to create many sheets of pastry separated by thin layers of butter.

I've taken into account the different properties of the gluten-free dough, which is unavoidably a little more delicate and lacks stretchiness. Rather than work with a single slab of butter, I create two, thin 'butter sheets' using many thin slices of butter. These slices are not overlapped but tessellated into the shape needed. This helps the process for two reasons.

Firstly, a butter slab is sturdier than the gluten-free dough, meaning that if you attempt to roll it out the 'normal' way, the dough splits and breaks around the butter. By keeping the butter thin and in pieces, the butter will move inside the dough rather than fight with it, allowing for it to be rolled without splitting.

Secondly, by using 2 thin layers of butter to begin the layering, we're creating a short cut in the lamination process. Our first fold creates 2 layers of butter between 3 sheets of dough, rather than 1 layer of butter between 2 sheets of dough. This means we can create the many layers needed with less rolling and folding. The less handling the gluten-free dough goes through at this stage the better, as the rolling process is labour-intensive and it's easy for the dough to become too warm, resulting in a tacky dough without proper layers.

*...continues overleaf*

## WORKING WITH YEAST

Yeast can be a finnicky ingredient, but the most common mistakes are pretty easily avoided! Below, I've included some key introductory information as well as some hints to get the best results in your yeasty bakes.

- **You should understand that yeast needs food to thrive – and it thrives on sugars.** When sugar is added to a dough, the yeast consumes the sugar and produces carbon dioxide. This is the gas that causes your baked goods to puff up. When you make a dough that includes yeast but little to no added sugar, the yeast will find other energy sources, such as the carbohydrates, in your starches. These are usually less efficient food sources, meaning less rise in your baked goods, but it also means a yeastier flavour, as the ratio of yeast to flour or starch has now been changed. You'll see that I always add some sugar to my yeasted bakes because gluten-free breads have a tendency towards being dense or tough. To give them the best chance of a nice rise and therefore a lighter, fluffier texture, a little sugar is necessary.

- **You should also be aware that salt can inhibit the growth of yeast, or even kill it.** You should therefore avoid direct contact between yeast and salt. You can do this easily just by ensuring you mix any added salt throughout the flour and other dry ingredients before you add the yeast, whether it be in dry form or as part of a liquid mixture of yeast and milk or water.

- **Yeast can also be sensitive to temperature.** An environment that is too cold will stunt its growth, while adding it to water or milk that is too hot will kill it. Where I've instructed that warm water or milk be used, you should aim for a temperature of 37–40°C (100–105°F). This is around the temperature of a bath for most people, so you can test it with your finger, but using a thermometer would reduce the margin of error. When in doubt, it's better for the liquid temperature to be a little too cool than too hot.

- **Temperature is also involved in proving.** In my recipes, you'll see directions to use a 'warm, draft-free place' to allow yeast to bloom or to prove doughs and shaped breads. If you have a warm, sunny room in your house, that can work (cover loosely with cling film/plastic wrap and then a tea towel/dish towel), but I find it easier to control proving conditions when using a smaller, enclosed space that will trap heat and humidity. The best solution I've found is to use my microwave:

Place a small cup of water in the microwave and microwave it for 1–2 minutes. Now add the bowl or tray of dough (covered loosely with cling film/plastic wrap and then a tea towel/dish towel) and close the door for the time specified in the recipe (do not turn the microwave on).

The microwave will hold some residual warmth from heating the water and the boiled water will continue to let off steam, producing more warmth and a good level of humidity. You can also do this in an oven (fill a small tray with boiling water from your kettle rather than using a cup). However, as your oven will often need to be preheated before your dough has finished proving, it's not always ideal. If the bowl or baking tray holding your dough is too big for your microwave (and especially if you bake a lot), you might prefer to invest in a large storage box to use as a proving space. You can then place the entire bowl/baking tray along with a cup of just-boiled water inside the box and seal with the lid, creating a warm, humid environment just as with the microwave method.

# CROISSANTS

Makes 3 large
or 6 small

**Day One**
110 g (4 oz) warm water (37–40°C/100–105°F is ideal)
1¾ teaspoons instant dried yeast
2 tablespoons caster (superfine) sugar
150 g (5¼ oz) **basic flour blend** (page 18)
1½ teaspoons psyllium husk powder
1 teaspoon xanthan gum
½ teaspoon gluten-free baking powder
⅓ teaspoon salt
1 egg
40 g (1½ oz) unsalted butter, chilled and cubed
1–2 teaspoons vegetable oil, for greasing

**Day Two**
120 g (4¼ oz) unsalted butter, chilled
**basic flour blend** (page 18), for dusting
1 egg yolk
2 tablespoons single (light) cream

**Day One**

MAKE THE DOUGH

Add the warm water to a medium jug or bowl, then mix in the yeast and 1 tablespoon of the sugar. Cover and leave in a warm, draft-free place for 10 minutes until the yeast has 'bloomed', which means there is a thick layer of foam on the surface. (If a layer of foam has not formed, your yeast may not be active and the croissants will not work properly. See page 36 for guidance on working with yeast.)

Meanwhile, in the bowl of a stand mixer, whisk together the remaining dry ingredients, including the remaining 1 tablespoon of sugar.

Whisk the egg into the water-yeast mixture, then pour this into the dry ingredients. Mix slowly (with the paddle attachment) until mostly combined, then mix vigorously (medium speed on a mixer) for 4–5 minutes, scraping down the side of the bowl once or twice to ensure all the ingredients are combining.

When the dough is smooth (it will still be quite wet and sticky), add the cubed butter, then run the mixer until no lumps of butter remain.

Grease a large bowl with the vegetable oil. Gently gather the dough into a ball in its current bowl, then carefully transfer it into the greased bowl. Shake and rotate the bowl a little to ensure the dough is a uniform ball, then flip it over. The aim is to have a smooth ball of dough that is greased all over, not to incorporate more fat into the dough, so try to avoid handling it and dimpling the dough with your fingers. Cover the bowl with cling film (plastic wrap) and refrigerate for 8–12 hours.

## Day Two

### PREPARE THE BUTTER FOR LAMINATING

Cut out two 11 × 24 cm (4¼ × 9½ in) sheets of baking paper. Slice the block of butter into very thin slices (about 2–3 mm/1⁄16–1⁄8 in) thick – I use a cheese slicer that resembles a vegetable peeler and it's perfect). Arrange the butter slices in an even layer onto each baking paper sheet. Do not overlap the butter slices; simply align them as evenly as possible over the entire surface of each sheet. If you need a little more butter, or a little less, that is perfectly fine. The important thing is to have two even sheets of thin butter slices measuring 11 × 24 cm (4¼ × 9½ in). Place them on a chopping board to keep them flat and refrigerate until needed.

### ENCLOSE THE BUTTER

Generously dust a large work surface with flour. Tip out the proved dough onto the surface and generously dust the dough with flour, too. Working gently but quickly, roll out the dough into a rectangle measuring 24 × 38 cm (9½ × 15 in). As you roll, move it around a little and dust with more flour as needed to stop it from sticking to the work surface. When it is rolled to size, position the dough so that a short edge is closest to you. Use a dry pastry brush to quickly brush away all excess flour from the surface of the dough.

Remove one of the baking paper sheets with butter from the fridge and lay this, butter side-down, 1–2 cm (½–¾ in) below the centre third of the dough. The short edges of baking paper should align with the longer edges of the dough. Gently press the butter into the dough just until it sticks, then peel the paper off and discard.

Fold the lower third of dough up and over the butter layer, aligning the edges as neatly as possible. Once again use the dry pastry brush to brush away the excess flour from this newly exposed layer of dough.

Place the second baking paper sheet of butter down onto the newly exposed layer of dough and repeat the process of gently compressing it, then peeling away the baking paper. Now fold the top third of the dough down over the second layer of butter, again lining up the edges as neatly as possible. Rotate the dough 90 degrees so that a short edge is once again closest to you.

### ROLL AND FOLD ONE

Flour the work surface again, then use your rolling pin to make lots of small lengthways dents over the dough. Now roll out the dough again into a rectangle measuring 24 × 38 cm (9½ × 15 in). As before, move it around a little and dust with more flour as needed to stop it from sticking to the work surface.

Using the dry pastry brush, brush away any flour from the surface of the dough, then repeat the folding process (this time without any butter sheets). Fold the lower third up and onto the centre third, brush away any flour, then fold the top third onto the newly exposed layer of dough. At this stage, if the dough is tacky or warm to the touch, cover and refrigerate it (keeping it flat) for 10–15 minutes.

...continues overleaf

## ROLL AND FOLD TWO

Ensure that a short edge of dough is once again closest to you. Roll out the dough again into a rectangle measuring 24 × 38 cm (9½ × 15 in), then repeat the brushing and folding process.

## ROLL AND FOLD THREE

Complete the rolling and folding once more, then cover and refrigerate for 15–20 minutes.

## FINAL ROLL

Prepare a large baking sheet lined with baking paper.

Roll out the dough once more, into a slightly larger rectangle measuring 28 × 40 cm (11 × 16 in). Move the dough around a little and dust with more flour as needed to stop it from sticking to the work surface.

## CUT AND SHAPE

Use a sharp knife to carefully trim away any rough dough edges, leaving you with a neat rectangle measuring about 26 × 38 cm (10¼ × 15 in).

Along the long edges of the dough, make marks spaced about 12.5 cm (5 in) apart, then cut along those lines to create 3 narrow rectangles of dough. Now make 1 cut diagonally along the length of each, creating 6 long, triangular pieces of dough.

Working with 1 piece at a time (and handling them gently), brush away excess flour from both sides of the triangle using the pastry brush. Position the narrow side of the triangle closest to you, then make a 2 cm (1 in) incision in the middle of this edge.

If you're making 6 smaller croissants, use your thumbs to curl the dough over onto itself, starting from the corners where you made the incision, then roll the dough into a croissant shape. Place this on the baking sheet, positioning it so that the 'tail' of the dough is held in place by the weight of croissant. Repeat with the remaining triangles of dough.

If you're making 3 larger croissants, use the same technique as above, but simply lay one triangle directly on top of another before you roll, doubling the amount of dough to be rolled.

As you roll the croissants, regardless of the size you have chosen, do not stretch the dough and do not apply too much pressure. You are not trying to seal the roll or combine the layers of dough. As you place them on the baking sheet, ensure they are spaced at least 6–7 cm (2½–2¾ in) apart.

...continues on page 44

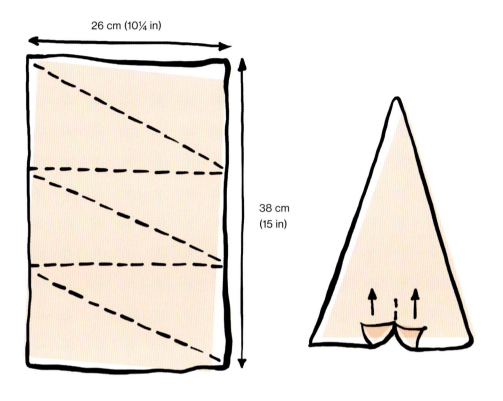
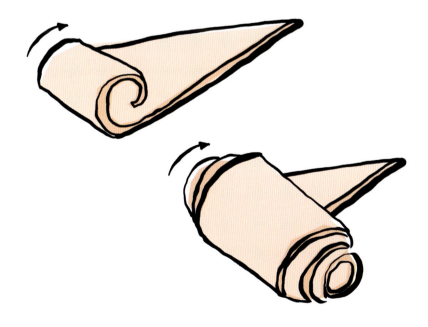

## PROVE AND PREP

Once all the croissants have been rolled, cover them loosely with cling film (plastic wrap), then leave to prove in a warm, draft-free place for 2–2.5 hours (see page 36 for proving tips).

When the croissants have proved for 1.5–2 hours, preheat the oven to 200°C Fan (400°F Fan) and prepare the egg wash by beating together the egg yolk and cream in a small bowl.

## BAKE

When the croissants are ready to bake, they will have grown about 75% in size. They should appear puffy, but not dimpled. If the croissants are dimpled, they may be overproved, which will affect their rise in the oven and the final texture, so keep a close eye on them (if they start to appear dimpled, end the proving period early).

Remove the cling film (plastic wrap) and use a pastry brush to gently brush them with egg wash. Apply the egg wash only to the uncut portions of dough; avoid the cut edges as much as possible as this can seal the layers closed, which will affect how the croissants rise. When all croissants have been coated in egg wash, transfer the baking sheet to the centre of your oven.

Bake the croissants for 5 minutes, then reduce the oven temperature to 160°C Fan (325°F Fan). Cook for a further 25 minutes, then reduce the oven temperature to 140°C Fan (285°F Fan). Cook for a further 20–25 minutes, until the pastries are a rich golden brown, then remove them from the oven and allow them to cool on the baking sheet for at least an hour before serving them.

# PAIN AU CHOCOLAT

Makes 6

These delicious pastries are the *crème de la crème* of my gluten-free cooking repertoire. Don't get me wrong, croissants are amazing and obviously the gold standard in terms of gluten-free baking, but when it comes to which pastry I'd choose for an indulgent treat, the pain au chocolat wins almost every time. The combo of buttery pastry and chocolate is just too good. The process of making these scrumptious morsels is the same as for croissants except for the final folding and shaping steps. I *highly* recommend starting with the introduction to croissants (page 34) before attempting these!

### Day One
110 g (4 oz) warm water (37–40°C/100–105°F is ideal)
1¾ teaspoons instant dried yeast
2 tablespoons caster (superfine) sugar
150 g (5¼ oz) **basic flour blend** (page 18)
1½ teaspoons psyllium husk powder
1 teaspoon xanthan gum
½ teaspoon gluten-free baking powder
⅓ teaspoon salt
1 egg
40 g (1½ oz) unsalted butter, chilled and cubed
1–2 teaspoons vegetable oil, for greasing

### Day Two
120 g (4¼ oz) unsalted butter, chilled
**basic flour blend** (page 18), for dusting
100 g (3½ oz) milk or dark cooking chocolate
1 egg yolk
2 tablespoons single (light) cream

### Day One
Follow all the Day One instructions for the croissants on page 38.

### Day Two
Follow the Day Two instructions for the croissants on pages 39–40 until you have completed 'roll and fold three'.

### FINAL ROLL
Prepare a large baking sheet lined with baking paper. Cut the chocolate into 12 batons that are 5–6 cm (2¼ in) long and 1 cm (½ in) wide (each pastry will contain 2 batons).

Roll out the dough once more, into a slightly larger rectangle measuring 28 × 40 cm (11 × 16 in). Move the dough around a little and dust with more flour as needed to stop it from sticking to the work surface.

...continues overleaf

## CUT AND SHAPE

Use a sharp knife to carefully trim away any rough dough edges, leaving you with a neat rectangle measuring about 26 × 38 cm (10¼ × 15 in).

Along the long edges of the dough, make marks spaced about 6–6.5 cm (2½ in) apart, then cut along those lines to create 6 narrow, rectangular strips of dough.

Working with 1 piece at a time (and handling them gently), brush away excess flour from both sides of the dough using a dry pastry brush. Place a single baton of chocolate along one of the short edges of the rectangle, then roll the dough just over it so it is encased in dough on all sides. Place a second baton of chocolate next to the rolled portion of dough, then continue rolling it up into a short log, encasing both pieces of chocolate in the middle. Place this on the lined baking sheet, positioning it so that the outer end of the dough strip is on the underside, pinned in place by the weight of the pastry. Repeat with the remaining dough strips and chocolate.

As you roll, do not stretch the dough and do not apply too much pressure. You are not trying to seal the roll or combine the layers of dough. As you place them on the baking sheet, ensure they are spaced at least 6–7 cm (2½–2¾ in) apart.

## PROVE AND PREP

Once all the pastries have been rolled, cover them loosely with cling film (plastic wrap), then leave to prove in a warm, draft-free place for 2–2.5 hours (see page 36 for proving tips).

When the croissants have proved for 1.5–2 hours, preheat the oven to 200°C Fan (400°F Fan) and prepare the egg wash by beating together the egg yolk and cream in a small bowl.

## BAKE

When the pastries are ready to bake, they will have grown about 75% in size. They should appear puffy, but not dimpled. If the pastries are dimpled, they may be overproved, which will affect their rise in the oven and the final texture, so keep a close eye on them (if they start to appear dimpled, end the proving period early).

Remove the cling film (plastic wrap) and use a pastry brush to gently brush them with egg wash. Apply the egg wash only to the uncut portions of dough; avoid the cut edges as much as possible as this can seal the layers closed, which will affect how the pastries rise. When all pastries have been coated in egg wash, transfer the baking sheet to the centre of your oven.

Bake the pastries for 5 minutes, then reduce the oven temperature to 160°C Fan (325°F Fan). Cook for a further 25 minutes, then reduce the oven temperature to 140°C Fan (285°F Fan). Cook for a further 20–25 minutes, until the pastries are a rich golden brown, then remove them from the oven and allow them to cool on the baking sheet for at least an hour before serving them.

# DIM SUM FEAST

Dim sum or yum cha – I've found that the
English term for this style of meal varies but it's generally
understood to be the same thing. It's a type of Chinese meal
often enjoyed in the morning consisting of many small plates
of utterly delicious food (usually served with steaming hot tea).
This can encompass a wide variety of savoury and sweet options, from
dumplings or noodles to sweet red bean pancakes or mango pudding.
For the most part, dim sum has been off-limits for people who can't eat
gluten – obviously when dumplings with wheat-based wrappers are a key
part of the meal, this poses a big problem, not to mention the other sources
of gluten hiding in nearly every dish. Happily, I've found ways to convert a
huge variety of my all-time favourite dim sum dishes! Some of these might
be new to you, others will be very familiar, but all of them are completely
delicious and perfect for a gluten-free dim sum feast. There are many,
many ways to fold dumplings, but you can also simply fold over and
seal the dumpling wrappers, so don't worry about needing to have
any technical skill – these recipes are accessible to everyone.
If you would like to get creative with your folding
and pleating, there are numerous videos online that
will show you how to do this.

# DUMPLING WRAPPERS

Makes 30–35

These dumpling wrappers have been my favourite recipe for years. They're really what started me off on my gluten-free cooking journey because I was so determined to get dumplings back into my life! It took years of experimenting, but I finally figured out a dough that can be rolled out really thinly, while still being soft and pliable.

135 g (⅓ oz) **dumpling flour blend** (page 19)
1 egg white
80 ml (2¾ fl oz) boiling water
rice flour, for dusting

Place the dumpling flour blend into a mixing bowl or the bowl of a food processor. You can also use a stand mixer fitted with a paddle attachment. Add the egg white and mix well to disperse it evenly through the flour.

While mixing, trickle in the boiling water. It will form a crumbly dough at first. Continue mixing and adding water until the dough comes together. If mixing by hand, tip the dough onto your work surface at this point and knead vigorously until it is smooth and slightly tacky, but not sticky. If using a food processor or stand mixer, mix until the dough is completely cleaning the side of the bowl. It should be soft, warm and pliable.

Separate the dough into two portions, rolling each into a neat ball. Seal one in a container or sandwich bag while you roll the first ball.

Use a rolling pin to flatten it to about 0.5 cm (¼ in) thick. If rolling by hand, continue to roll the dough out with the rolling pin, dusting the dough with rice flour only as necessary, until it is about 1 mm (¹⁄₁₆ in) thick.

Alternatively, use a pasta machine/roller. Once the dough is about 0.5 cm (¼ in) thick, lightly dust it on both sides with rice flour and start passing it through the roller on the widest setting. The first time you pass it through, it may come out a little scraggly with rough edges but, don't worry, you can fold the dough up, roll it back out with a rolling pin and pass it through the pasta roller again. Work your way through the roller settings, until you end up with a neat, thin sheet of dough (the 4th or 5th setting on the pasta roller).

Now fold the sheet up neatly so that the new, straight edges are about the same width as the roller. Set the roller to the widest setting again, then work your way through the roller settings again, until the dough is 1–1.5 mm (¹⁄₁₆ in) thick (the 5th or 6th setting on the pasta roller). If the dough becomes too dry during this process, moisten your fingers with a little water and run them over the dough sheet, then fold up the dough and pass it through the roller again.

When you have a thin sheet of dough, dust it with more rice flour and cut out circles using an 8–9 cm (1¼–3½ in) cookie cutter (you can also use a knife to cut it into square wrappers).

Any scraps of dough can be gathered and remixed with a little trickle of boiling water, then re-rolled. Do note that repeated re-rolling will create a tougher, slightly more brittle dough if you're adding lots of rice flour as you go.

The finished dumpling wrappers can be dusted with rice flour and stacked, then stored in an airtight bag or container until use.

Repeat with the second ball of dough.

## STORAGE

If the wrappers are not being used within the hour, store the bag or container in the fridge for up to 3 days. Allow them to come to room temperature before use.

You can also freeze the dumpling wrappers for up to 2 months. Wrap the stack in paper towel, then seal in an airtight container or bag. Before use, thaw them completely in the fridge and then allow them to come to room temperature. You may need to wrap them in a new sheet of paper towel as they thaw, as too much moisture from thawing will make them soggy.

Alternatively, you can also freeze filled and folded dumplings. Arrange them in a single layer on a tray or plate dusted with rice flour. Freeze them solid, then transfer them to a bag or container for easy storage. Cook directly from frozen for a couple more minutes than the stated cook time.

## NOTES

*This recipe makes 30–35 wrappers but that does depend a bit on your rolling and cutting technique. If you roll to thickness of 1 mm (1/16 in) and keep re-rolling and cutting until you use all the scraps, you'll get a few more. If you leave them thicker and don't use all the dough, you'll get fewer, so bear that in mind.*

*You can also make these egg free, with a small adjustment. Add ½ teaspoon of xanthan gum and 1 teaspoon psyllium husk powder to the dumpling flour blend (to replace the egg) and increase the quantity of boiling water to 130ml (4 1/3 fl oz). You can also use this dough to make egg-free noodles!*

# WONTON WRAPPERS

### Makes 30-40

This is another variety of dumpling wrapper using my trusty dumpling flour blend. These wrappers can be rolled super thin, and they have an even silkier texture than the slightly hardier dumpling wrappers (page 52), making them ideal for boiled wontons (wonton soup, anyone?) or delicate siu mai (page 71). They're also very versatile and hold up well when deep-fried to become light and crispy! Just make sure that if you're frying them, your filling is relatively dry, as a particularly juicy filling will stop them staying crisp for very long.

110 g (4 oz) **dumpling flour blend** (page 19)
1 tablespoon psyllium husk powder
1 egg, plus 1 egg yolk
1 teaspoon neutral oil (vegetable or rapeseed/canola)
3–4 tablespoons boiling water
rice flour, for dusting

Place the dumpling flour blend and psyllium husk into a mixing bowl or the bowl of a food processor. You can also use a stand mixer fitted with a paddle attachment. Whisk together the whole egg, egg yolk and oil, then pour this into the dry ingredients, mixing well until combined.

While mixing, trickle in the boiling water. It will form a crumbly dough at first. Continue mixing and adding water until the dough comes together. If mixing by hand, tip the dough onto your work surface at this point and knead vigorously until it is smooth and slightly tacky, but not sticky. If using a food processor or stand mixer, mix until the dough is completely cleaning the side of the bowl. It should be soft, warm and pliable.

Separate the dough into two portions, rolling each into a neat ball. Seal one in a container or sandwich bag while you roll the first ball.

Use a rolling pin to flatten it to about 0.5 cm (¼ in) thick. If rolling by hand, continue to roll the dough out with the rolling pin, dusting the dough with rice flour only as necessary, until it is about 1 mm (¹⁄₁₆ in) thick.

Alternatively, use a pasta machine/roller, once the dough is about 0.5 cm (¼ in) thick, lightly dust it on both sides with rice flour and start passing it through the roller on the widest setting. The first time you pass it through, it may come out a little scraggly with rough edges but, don't worry, you can fold the dough up, roll it back out with a rolling pin and pass it through the pasta roller again. Work your way through the roller settings, until you end up with a neat, thin sheet of dough (the 4th or 5th setting on the pasta roller).

Now fold the sheet up neatly so that the new, straight edges are about the same width as the roller. Set the roller to the widest setting again, then work your way through the roller settings again, until the dough is 0.8–1 mm (less than ¹⁄₁₆ in) thick (the 6th or 7th setting on the pasta roller). If the dough becomes too dry during this process, moisten your fingers with a little water and run them over the dough sheet, then fold up the dough and pass it through the roller again.

When you have a thin sheet of dough, dust it with more rice flour and use a sharp knife to cut it into 8–9 cm (1¼–3½ in) squares. You can also use a round cookie cutter if you prefer.

Any scraps of dough can be gathered and remixed with a little trickle of boiling water, then re-rolled. Do note that repeated re-rolling will create a tougher, slightly more brittle dough if you're adding lots of rice flour as you go.

The finished wonton wrappers can be dusted with rice flour and stacked, then stored in an airtight bag or container until use.

Repeat with the second ball of dough.

## STORAGE

If the wrappers are not being used within the hour, store the bag or container in the fridge for up to 3 days. Allow them to come to room temperature before use.

You can also freeze the wonton wrappers for up to 2 months. Wrap the stack in paper towel, then seal in an airtight container or bag. Before use, thaw them completely in the fridge and then allow them to come to room temperature. You may need to wrap them in a new sheet of paper towel as they thaw, as too much moisture from thawing will make them soggy.

Alternatively, you can also freeze filled and folded wontons. Arrange them in a single layer on a tray or plate dusted with rice flour. Freeze them solid, then transfer them to a bag or container for easy storage. Cook directly from frozen for a couple more minutes than the stated cook time.

# CHIVE AND PORK BELLY DUMPLINGS

*Makes about 40*

**These are my take on a classic pork and chive dumpling. They're meaty, aromatic and completely delicious. Taking the time to hand-mince pork belly for this filling is a slightly more laborious task than using pre-prepared minced (ground) pork, but pork belly has a higher fat ratio than most minced (ground) pork available in the supermarket, which ensures these dumplings are juicy and flavourful!**

1 quantity of **dumpling wrappers** (page 52), cut into circles
tapioca starch or rice flour, for dusting
1–2 tablespoons neutral oil
your choice of dipping sauce, to serve

**For the filling**
300 g (10½ oz) pork belly
45 g (1¾ oz) Chinese chives (garlic chives), finely chopped
4 garlic cloves, minced
3 teaspoons grated fresh ginger
1½ teaspoons sesame oil
2 teaspoons gluten-free soy sauce
1½ teaspoons rice vinegar
1½ teaspoons mirin
¾ teaspoon caster (superfine) sugar
1½ teaspoons gluten-free cornflour (cornstarch)
1½ tablespoons water
¾ teaspoon gluten-free chicken powder (or ½ teaspoon salt)
pinch of white pepper

Finely chop and then mince the pork belly. You can use a food processor for this but be careful not to take it too far. The mince should hold together when squeezed, but you should still be able to distinguish between small pieces of pork. Transfer to a mixing bowl.

Add the rest of the filling ingredients to the bowl and mix well.

To fold the dumplings, place a small spoonful of the filling into the centre of a wrapper. Lightly moisten your finger with water and run it over one side of the wrapper. It should become slightly sticky. (If it's wet and slippery, you've used too much water. Simply let it dry slightly before folding and/or dust your fingertips with tapioca starch or rice flour to prevent the wrapper from getting soggy.) Fold the wrapper in half over the filling and press the dry side onto the moistened side to seal. You can pleat as you go or leave it as a simple semi-circle. Repeat with the rest of the filling and wrappers, then place the folded dumplings on a tray lightly dusted with tapioca starch or rice flour.

To cook the dumplings, heat the neutral oil in a large non-stick frying pan (skillet) set over medium heat. Place the dumplings into the pan, with the sealed edge pointing upwards, and cover with the lid. Fry for 3–4 minutes until the bases of the dumplings have browned, then pour 60–70 ml (4–5 tablespoons) of water all around the pan and quickly replace the lid.

Allow them to steam for 3–4 minutes until the tops of the dumplings looked cooked through, then remove the lid and allow any excess water in the pan to evaporate. After another 2–3 minutes, the dumplings will be cooked in the middle and the bases should have crisped up again.

Transfer to a large plate and serve with your choice of dipping sauce.

# CHICKEN AND SHIITAKE DUMPLINGS

*Makes about 40*

Chicken dumplings are not usually my go-to as I find them less flavourful than dumplings with a richer filling. That is, until I paired chicken with shiitake mushrooms. They make these dumplings rich and luxurious, and by adding some of the mushroom soaking liquid to bind the filling together, I make sure that the mushroom flavour complements every single bite!

1 quantity of **dumpling wrappers** (page 52), cut into circles
tapioca starch or rice flour, for dusting
1–2 tablespoons neutral oil
your choice of dipping sauce, to serve

**For the filling**
6 dried shiitake mushrooms
500 g (18 oz) minced (ground) chicken
3 spring onions (scallions), finely chopped
2 teaspoons grated fresh ginger
3 garlic cloves, minced
½ tablespoon sesame oil
½ tablespoon gluten-free oyster sauce
1 tablespoon gluten-free soy sauce
½ teaspoon caster (superfine) sugar
¼ teaspoon white pepper
1 teaspoon gluten-free chicken powder (or ½ teaspoon salt)
2 teaspoons tapioca starch
1 tablespoon lard

Place the dried shiitake mushrooms in a small heatproof bowl and cover them with boiling water. Set aside to soak for at least 10 minutes while you prepare the rest of the filling.

In a large bowl, mix the chicken mince with the rest of the filling ingredients. Once softened, add 2 tablespoons of the mushroom soaking liquid to the chicken mixture, then drain and gently squeeze the mushrooms to remove any excess liquid. Finely chop the mushrooms, then add them to the chicken mixture and mix well.

To fold the dumplings, place a small spoonful of the filling into the centre of a wrapper. Lightly moisten your finger with water and run it over one side of the wrapper. It should become slightly sticky. (If it's wet and slippery, you've used too much water. Simply let it dry slightly before folding and/or dust your fingertips with tapioca starch or rice flour to prevent the wrapper from getting soggy.) Fold the wrapper in half over the filling and press the dry side onto the moistened side to seal. You can pleat as you go or leave it as a simple semi-circle. Repeat with the rest of the filling and wrappers, then place the folded dumplings on a tray lightly dusted with tapioca starch or rice flour.

To cook the dumplings, heat the neutral oil in a large non-stick frying pan (skillet) set over medium heat. Place the dumplings into the pan, with the sealed edge pointing upwards, and cover with the lid. Fry for 3–4 minutes until the bases of the dumplings have browned, then pour 60–70 ml (4–5 tablespoons) of water all around the pan and quickly replace the lid.

Steam for 3–4 minutes until the tops of the dumplings looked cooked through, then remove the lid and allow any excess water in the pan to evaporate. After another 2–3 minutes, the dumplings will be cooked in the middle and the bases should have crisped up again.

Transfer to a large plate and serve with your choice of dipping sauce.

# SALT AND PEPPER SQUID TENTACLES

Serves 2–3

I feel that a dim sum meal isn't quite complete without at least one fried dish, and these squid tentacles are a fantastic option. The stir-fried aromatics work beautifully with the squid and the crispy texture makes them a delicious snack on their own, or the perfect complement to the array of steamed and softer foods that make up this feast.

neutral oil, for frying
2 garlic cloves, finely chopped
2 shallots, finely chopped
2 fresh red chillies, finely sliced
2 dried Sichuan chillies
½ teaspoon caster (superfine) sugar
¼ teaspoon white pepper
¼–½ teaspoon salt, to taste
100 g (3½ oz) gluten-free cornflour (cornstarch)
2 spring onions (scallions), finely sliced

**For the squid**
250 g (9 oz) squid tentacles, cleaned and cut into bite-sized pieces (if using baby squid tentacles, these can remain whole)
1 teaspoon gluten-free soy sauce
1 teaspoon gluten-free oyster sauce
1 teaspoon sesame oil
1 tablespoon gluten-free cornflour (cornstarch)
¼ teaspoon white pepper

Start by marinating the squid tentacles. Place them in a small bowl along with all the other ingredients, then mix well to coat and set aside.

In a large frying pan (skillet) or wok set over medium heat, heat 1 tablespoon of neutral oil, then add the garlic, shallots and fresh and dried chillies. Stir fry for 1–2 minutes until the shallot has softened, then add the sugar, white pepper and salt. Toss to combine, then take the pan off the heat and place to one side.

To a large saucepan, add 5–7.5 cm (2–3 in) neutral oil and set over medium-high heat. The oil is hot enough when a wooden chopstick or wooden spoon handle sizzles when dipped into the oil.

Place the cornflour in a bowl then, one-by-one, dunk the squid tentacles into it to completely coat them.

Working in batches, carefully drop the squid tentacles into the hot oil. Don't overcrowd the pan or agitate them as they cook as this will prevent them from cooking evenly and might dislodge the coating. Fry for about 2 minutes, or until crispy, then remove from the pan with a slotted spoon and allow the squid to drain on a plate lined with paper towel. Allow the oil to reheat slightly before frying the next batch of squid.

Once all the squid is cooked, place the wok with the aromatics back over high heat until sizzling. Add the fried squid and spring onions, then toss briefly to combine everything.

Transfer to a serving dish and serve.

### NOTE

*You can also make a vegan version of these by replacing the squid with the same quantity of enoki mushrooms. Simply cut off the root section of the mushrooms and pull the bunch apart into 1-2 cm (½–¾ in) sections. Then proceed with the recipe as above.*

# PRAWN CHEUNG FUN

### Makes 4 rolls

Cheung fun are a type of fresh rice noodle that is steamed to form wide, thin sheets, filled with various savoury fillings and doused in flavourful sauces. They can be tricky to steam on the stovetop, so I make mine in the microwave! It's a simpler method that means they turn out perfectly every time. These prawn cheung fun are my favourite but you can also use youtiao (page 81) to fill them, for another classic take on this dim sum dish.

**For the prawns**
12 prawns (shrimp), peeled and deveined
¼ teaspoon gluten-free chicken powder (or ⅛ teaspoon salt)
⅛ teaspoon salt
¼ teaspoon white pepper
¼ teaspoon caster (superfine) sugar
½ teaspoon tapioca starch
½ teaspoon sesame oil

**For the cheung fun**
75 g (2¾ oz) rice flour
35 g (1¼ oz) tapioca starch
250 ml (8½ fl oz) warm water
⅛ teaspoon salt
1 teaspoon sesame oil
1–2 tablespoons neutral oil

**For the sauce**
½ teaspoon gluten-free oyster sauce
1½ teaspoons gluten-free soy sauce
½ teaspoon rice vinegar
¼ teaspoon caster (superfine) sugar

**To serve**
chilli oil
spring onions (scallions), finely sliced

Prepare the prawns by combining them in a small bowl with all the other ingredients to marinate for 5 minutes. Lay the prawns in a single layer in a lined steamer basket or tray, then steam over medium heat for 2–3 minutes until just cooked through. Set aside.

Meanwhile, prepare the cheung fun batter by whisking together all the ingredients (except the neutral oil) in a mixing bowl until smooth. It should be a very thin batter.

Liberally brush a large, flat-bottomed, microwave-safe dish with the neutral oil. I use a baking dish measuring approximately 18 × 24 cm (7 × 9½ in).

Pour just enough of the cheung fun batter into the dish to evenly cover the base – about 80 ml (5½ tablespoons) of batter is perfect for the baking dish I use. It should be 1–2 mm (1/16 in) thick. Place in the microwave and cook on high heat (900W) for 2 minutes. If, after 2 minutes, the batter isn't quite set all over, cook for 1 further minute.

Remove from the microwave and use a silicone spatula to gently loosen the edges of the noodle from the baking dish. Lay 3 prawns along a short edge of the noodle, then roll the noodle into a log with the prawns inside. Transfer to a serving plate. Repeat with the rest of the batter and prawns, brushing the dish with a little more oil before cooking the next noodle, until you have 4 rolls.

Once you've made your cheung fun, make the sauce. Combine the sauce ingredients in a small saucepan over medium heat and stir until the sugar has just dissolved.

Spoon the sauce over the cheung fun, then top with chilli oil and finely sliced spring onion.

# XIAO LONG BAO (SOUP DUMPLINGS)

*Makes about 30*

I'm not sure I've ever met anyone who didn't like these. If you haven't had them before, your first guess might be that they're dumplings served in soup. However, that's the fun surprise – the soup is contained within the dumplings themselves! This is done by including a gelatinised broth with the meat filling – when they're heated during cooking, the broth liquifies and is held within the dumpling. Although this broth is traditionally simmered for hours so that it gelatinises with the collagen from bones, I use gelatine powder here as a handy shortcut!

1 quantity of **dumpling wrappers** (page 52), cut into circles
tapioca starch or rice flour, for dusting
your choice of dipping sauce, to serve

**For the meat filling**
300 g (10½ oz) minced (ground) pork
2 teaspoons pork lard (at room temperature)
2 spring onions (scallions), finely chopped
2 teaspoons grated fresh ginger
3 garlic cloves, minced
2½ teaspoons gluten-free soy sauce
2 teaspoons gluten-free oyster sauce
1 teaspoon sesame oil
1 teaspoon gluten-free Shaoxing rice wine (or other cooking wine)
½ teaspoon caster (superfine) sugar
½ teaspoon gluten-free chicken powder (or ¼ teaspoon salt)
⅛ teaspoon white pepper

**For the gelatinised stock**
200 ml (6¾ fl oz) beef stock
2 teaspoons gelatine powder
pinch of white pepper
½ teaspoon sesame oil
½ teaspoon gluten-free chicken powder (or ¼ teaspoon salt)

Begin by making the gelatinised stock that will form the soup part of these soup dumplings. If you're using a stock cube with boiling water, add the gelatine straight into the stock while very hot and stir to dissolve. If using ready-made stock, heat the stock in a saucepan to a simmer, then remove from the heat and stir in the gelatine powder. Add the white pepper, sesame oil, chicken powder and stir well. Pour the stock mixture into a shallow dish and cover with cling film (plastic wrap). One cool, place in the fridge for 2–3 hours to set completely.

To make the meat filling, mix the pork mince and lard in a bowl to break up the lard. Add the remaining filling ingredients, then mix again until everything is evenly combined.

While still in the dish, use a knife to cut the set stock into small cubes. There's no need to be precise, you just want to be able to mix the set stock throughout the meat filling. Once cut, mix all the stock with the meat filling.

To fold the dumplings, place a small spoonful of the filling into the centre of a wrapper. Lightly moisten your finger with water and run it around the edge of the wrapper. It should become slightly sticky. (If it's wet and slippery, you've used too much water. Simply let it dry slightly before folding and/or dust your fingertips with tapioca starch or rice flour to prevent the wrapper from getting soggy.) Bring the edges of the dumpling together on top of the filling, like a little sack or money bag (the dumpling needs to be sealed at the top so that the broth doesn't leak as they cook). Repeat with the rest of the filling and wrappers.

In batches, place the dumplings in a lined steamer basket, spaced 2–3 cm (¾–1¼ in) apart, and steam over medium heat for 11–12 minutes. Serve hot with dipping sauce.

# STIR-FRIED SHREDDED POTATOES

Serves 4–6

**This is an addictive vegetable dish often found on dim sum menus. The julienned potatoes have a very pleasant texture and eating them is a little like eating noodles. This dish is typically quite spicy, but you can customise the spice level by adjusting the amount of chillies and chilli oil I've suggested here.**

2 large potatoes (about 650 g/23 oz total weight), peeled
1 tablespoon neutral oil
3 dried Sichuan chillies
1 teaspoon Sichuan peppercorns
2 garlic cloves, finely chopped
1 tablespoon sesame oil
1 teaspoon rice vinegar
1 tablespoon chilli oil (optional)
½–1 teaspoon salt (to taste)

Fill a large bowl two-thirds full with water and ice cubes. Slice each peeled potato along the longest edge into large oval-shaped discs, 2–3 mm ($1/16$–$1/8$ in) thick. Stack these, then slice them into matchsticks, again along the longest edge. You should end up with lots of thin sticks of potato, as if you're making very thin French fries.

Place the julienned potatoes into the ice bath for 30–40 minutes, then drain thoroughly. This removes the starch from the surface of the cut potatoes and helps them retain their texture when cooking.

After 30 minutes, heat the neutral oil in a large frying pan (skillet) or wok set over medium heat. Add the dried Sichuan chillies and stir fry until they start to darken in colour. Next add the peppercorns and garlic and fry, stirring constantly, for about 20 seconds.

Add the potatoes to the wok along with 2 tablespoons of water. Stir fry for 4–6 minutes until the potatoes have wilted and are cooked through, while still retaining a slight bite.

As they finish cooking, turn the heat up to high and add the sesame oil, rice vinegar, chilli oil (if you like) and salt to taste. Stir fry for another 30 seconds or so, then transfer to a serving dish and enjoy while piping hot.

# PRAWN AND PORK SIU MAI

### Makes about 20

Siu mai are one of my favourite dumplings to make because their folding technique is one of the easiest to learn. They're also usually filled with a delicious combination of prawn and pork, which means you get the best of both worlds in terms of flavour – meaty richness from the pork and the delicate mild bite of succulent prawn.

200 g (7 oz) prawns (shrimp), peeled and deveined
175 g (6¼ oz) pork belly, minced
2 spring onions (scallions), finely chopped
3 garlic cloves, minced
2 teaspoons grated fresh ginger
½ teaspoon caster (superfine) sugar
⅛ teaspoon white pepper
1 teaspoon sesame oil
1 teaspoon gluten-free soy sauce
½ teaspoon gluten-free chicken powder (or ¼ teaspoon salt)
1 teaspoon sake (or other rice wine)
2 tablespoons gluten-free cornflour (cornstarch)
1 quantity of **wonton wrappers** (page 56), cut into squares
your choice of dipping sauce, to serve

Start by roughly chopping up the prawns. There's no need to mince them – some texture from larger pieces is ideal – but the filling will hold together best if the prawns are chopped fairly small. Add the chopped prawns to a mixing bowl along with all the other ingredients (except the wonton wrappers) and mix very well until the proteins in the pork have broken down significantly. You will know the filling is ready when you can't discern individual pieces of pork and the filling is sticky.

To fold the siu mai, place a generous spoonful of filling into the centre of the wonton wrapper, pressing it into the wrapper and spreading it around slightly. Now bring the edges of the wrapper up around the filling in a bucket-like shape, with the filling exposed at the top. If necessary, moisten the outside of the wrapper so that any excess folds of dough stick to the rest of the wrapper. You can also place the siu mai on your work surface and apply pressure from the top to compact and shape the dumpling. It should be able to stand upright – some excess wrapper at the top is perfectly fine.

In batches, place the siu mai in a lined steamer basket, spaced 1–2 cm (½–¾ in) apart, and steam over medium heat for 11–12 minutes.

Serve hot with your favourite dipping sauce

### NOTE

*As with some of my other pork dumplings, I prefer to mince my own pork belly for these, just because the fattier cut makes for a juicier dumpling. However, you can substitute minced (ground) pork for convenience if you wish (in which case, I'd recommend adding 1–2 teaspoons of pork lard).*

# PRAWN AND SCALLOP HAR GOW

*Makes about 40*

Har gow or har gau are a staple on any dim sum menu and popular for good reason. They are made with a slightly chewier, softer wrapper than most other dumplings and are usually filled with succulent prawns delicately flavoured with aromatics.

300 g (10½ oz) prawns (shrimp), peeled and deveined
80 g (2¾ oz) raw scallops (with roe removed)
1 spring onion (scallion), finely chopped
60 g (2¼ oz) canned water chestnuts, drained and finely chopped
2 garlic cloves, minced
2 teaspoons grated fresh ginger
1½ teaspoons sesame oil
1 teaspoon gluten-free soy sauce
1 teaspoon gluten-free oyster sauce
1 teaspoon sake (or other rice wine)
½ teaspoon gluten-free chicken powder (or ¼ teaspoon salt)
½ teaspoon caster (superfine) sugar
¼ teaspoon white pepper
3 teaspoons gluten-free cornflour (cornstarch)
3 teaspoons finely grated black truffle (optional)
your choice of chilli oil, to serve

**For the har gow dumpling wrappers**
200 g (7 oz) **dumpling flour blend** (page 19)
80 g (2¾ oz) glutinous rice flour, plus extra for dusting
2 egg whites
160 ml (5½ fl oz) boiling water

Roughly chop half the prawns and all the scallops, then add them to a mixing bowl. Now very finely chop (mince) the rest of the prawns and add these to the bowl, too. Add all the remaining ingredients (except the chilli oil) along with 1 teaspoon of cold water and mix well until combined. Cover and store in the fridge while you make the dumpling wrappers.

In another mixing bowl, combine the dumpling flour with the glutinous rice flour. Stir the egg whites through the flour, then, while mixing constantly, trickle in the freshly boiled water.

When a scraggly dough has formed, tip it onto the work surface and knead by hand while it is still very warm. It will likely stick to your work surface initially but as you work the dough, it will become more pliable. (Alternatively, you can mix and knead the dough in a food processor.)

When the dough is smooth and slightly tacky but not sticky, roll it into a ball. Dust your work surface with glutinous rice flour, then use a rolling pin to roll out the dough into a sheet 2–3 mm (¹⁄₁₆–⅛ in) thick, continuing to dust it as necessary to prevent it from sticking. (Alternatively, you can use a pasta machine/roller to roll the dough to the correct thickness.)

Use a 10 cm (4 in) round cookie cutter to cut out the dumpling wrappers, then stack them with plenty of glutinous rice flour dusted between each one. Gather, knead (with a little extra water if necessary) and re-roll the dough scraps so you can cut out more wrappers.

To fold the dumplings, place a teaspoonful of the filling into the centre of a wrapper. Lightly moisten your finger with water and run it over one side of the wrapper. It should become slightly sticky. (If it's wet and slippery, you've used too much water. Simply let it dry slightly before folding and/or dust your fingertips with glutinous rice flour to prevent the wrapper from getting soggy.) Fold the wrapper in half over the filling and press the dry side onto the moistened side to seal. You can pleat as you go or leave it as a simple semi-circle. Repeat with the rest of the filling and wrappers, then place the folded dumplings on a tray lightly dusted with glutinous rice flour.

In batches, place the dumplings in a lined steamer basket, spaced 1–2 cm (½–¾ in) apart, and steam over medium heat for 11–12 minutes.

Serve hot with dipping sauce – I highly recommend using your favourite chilli oil.

NOTES

*The wrappers I've made are not exactly like traditional har gow wrappers as those are very hands-on to make (each wrapper needs to be rolled individually). Instead, I've adapted my regular wrapper recipe (page 52) to be more like those used for har gow, while still being quite easy to roll out in a single sheet from which the wrappers can be cut. This makes them more beginner-friendly and easier to make in bulk!*

*I add scallops to my filling to make the dumplings meaty and luxurious, but you can absolutely leave out the scallops and simply use 80 g (2¾ oz) more prawns. My other lavish addition is fresh black truffle. This is definitely not essential as truffles can be expensive and hard to find, but the flavour combination of prawns, scallop and truffle really is divine so I highly recommend you give this a go at least once!*

# HAKKA-STYLE STUFFED TOFU

Serves 2–3

**This dish is one I was only introduced to after my coeliac disease diagnosis, as it can be made gluten free with only a few simple modifications. It's an ideal option if you're craving the flavours of dumplings or dim sum but don't have the time (or energy) to make dumpling wrappers from scratch. If you're not having this as part of a bigger dim sum spread, served with some steamed rice and greens it'll become a satisfying meal, comfortably feeding two people.**

120 g (4¼ oz) prawns (shrimp), peeled and deveined (about 8–10 medium-sized prawns)
½ teaspoon grated fresh ginger
1 small spring onion (scallion), finely chopped, plus extra to serve
1 garlic clove, minced
¼ teaspoon salt
⅛ teaspoon white pepper
⅛ teaspoon caster (superfine) sugar
½ teaspoon gluten-free gluten-free cornflour (cornstarch), plus 1–2 teaspoons extra for dusting
350 g (12½ oz) block firm silken tofu

**For the sauce**
2 teaspoons gluten-free soy sauce
1 teaspoon gluten-free oyster sauce
80 ml (2¾ fl oz) water
¼ teaspoon sesame oil
1 teaspoon cornflour (cornstarch)

Finely chop the prawns and place them in a mixing bowl. Add the ginger, spring onion, garlic, salt, pepper, sugar and cornflour and mix well to combine. Cover and set aside.

Slice the tofu into blocks, each about 2.5 cm (1 in) thick. Place the pieces onto a heatproof plate (or plates) that will fit into your steamer.

Use a small spoon or melon baller to carefully scoop away the centre of each piece of tofu, without going the whole way through. The sides and base of the tofu should remain intact but there should be a sizeable hollow in each piece. Transfer the scooped-out tofu to the bowl with the prawns and mix very well.

Using a fine sieve, dust a little cornflour evenly over the hollowed-out tofu pieces. Spoon the prawn and tofu filling into the hollow of each piece of tofu. You can pack each piece quite generously. Transfer the plate(s) to a steamer basket and allow to steam over medium heat for 8–9 minutes.

While the stuffed tofu is steaming, make the sauce. In a small saucepan, whisk together all the sauce ingredients, then place over medium heat. Allow it to cook for 3–4 minutes until it has thickened and there is no floury taste.

Transfer the cooked stuffed tofu to a serving plate, then top generously with the sauce and extra spring onion before serving.

NOTE

*I use a rectangular block of silken tofu but you can also use the round, sausage-shaped silken tofu. If so, simply cut in into 2.5 cm (1 in) thick rounds instead or rectangles.*

# BEAN CURD ROLLS

### Serves 2–3

While these are not dumplings, they're a popular dim sum option that is prepared in quite a similar way – with a flavourful meaty filling encased in a wrapping to be cooked. However, in this case, the wrapper is made from tofu skin. This is a common ingredient in Chinese cooking but it is yet to become a staple in Western supermarkets in the same way fresh tofu has. Tofu skin is traditionally made from boiling soy milk – as the soy milk heats, a skin forms on the surface. This is carefully peeled away and then hung up or spread out to dry. It can be purchased quite readily from Asian grocers, usually as a frozen fresh product or as a dried pantry ingredient. I prefer to use the dried variety as this has a long shelf life and can be kept handy for whenever I want a dim sum fix!

1 packet (about 200 g/7 oz) tofu skin sheets
1½ tablespoons gluten-free cornflour (cornstarch) mixed with 1 tablespoon water to form a slurry
neutral oil, for shallow frying
1 spring onion (scallion), finely sliced
chilli oil, to serve (optional)

**For the filling**
4 dried shiitake mushrooms
250 g (9 oz) minced (ground) pork
1 small carrot, peeled and grated
70 g (2½ oz) canned water chestnuts, drained and chopped
2 spring onions (scallions), finely chopped
1½ teaspoons grated fresh ginger
2 teaspoons gluten-free oyster sauce
2 teaspoons gluten-free soy sauce
1 teaspoon sesame oil
⅛ teaspoon white pepper
¼ teaspoon caster (superfine) sugar
1 tablespoon gluten-free cornflour (cornstarch)

**For the sauce**
1½ teaspoons gluten-free soy sauce
1½ teaspoons gluten-free oyster sauce
120 ml (4 fl oz) water
1 teaspoon sesame oil
pinch of white pepper
2 teaspoons gluten-free cornflour (cornstarch)

Start by rehydrating the dried tofu skin sheets (if you're working with the frozen variety, simply allow them to thaw – they should be soft enough to roll without snapping or cracking). Fill a large bowl or tub with room-temperature water, then lower in the tofu skin sheets. Allow them to soak until they're soft and pliable (the time it takes will depend on the brand – they will need to soak anywhere from 2–8 minutes – so go by texture), then carefully remove them from the water and spread them out on a clean tea towel (dish towel). Cover them with a second tea towel to stop them drying out as you prepare the filling.

Now prepare the filling. Place the dried shiitake mushrooms in a small heatproof bowl and cover them with boiling water. Allow to sit for at least 10 minutes while you prepare the other ingredients.

In a mixing bowl, combine all the remaining filling ingredients and mix well.

When soft, drain the mushrooms and squeeze out any excess liquid with your hands. Finely chop them and add to the bowl of filling. Mix well until the filling mixture is sticky.

Uncover the tofu skin sheets and use a clean, moist cloth to wipe both sides of every sheet. They can be quite salty, so this helps to remove any excess salt. Cut the sheets into roughly 15 × 21 cm (6 × 8¼ in) rectangles (about the size of an A5 piece of paper).

Working with one tofu skin sheet at a time, place about 2 tablespoons of filling along the short edge of the sheet. Roll it up tightly then use some of the cornflour slurry to seal the end. Repeat with the rest of the tofu skin sheets and filling.

Place 1 cm (½ in) of neutral oil in a deep frying pan (skillet) and set it over medium heat. Check the oil temperature – when you're ready to fry, it should be hot enough that a wooden chopstick or wooden spoon sizzles when dipped into the oil. Place the bean curd rolls into the oil, seam side-down and fry for 2–3 minutes, rotating them regularly, until crisp and golden on all sides. Transfer to a plate lined with paper towels to absorb any excess oil.

Next, place the rolls on a heatproof plate (or plates) that will fit into your steamer basket, then steam over medium-high heat for 10 minutes.

Meanwhile, whisk together the sauce ingredients in a small saucepan, then place it over medium heat. Allow to cook for 3–4 minutes until the sauce has thickened and there is no floury taste.

Remove the bean curd rolls from the steamer and top them generously with the sauce. Serve sprinkled with spring onion and with chilli oil for dipping (if you like).

# STEAMED PORK BUNS TAKE 12 (CHAR SIU BAO)

*Makes 6*

When I develop recipes, they always start out as handwritten drafts in my notebook, and each one is titled. Where I have to make something twice or three times, it will be re-written and renamed with 'Take 2' or 'Take 3' added to the title, so that I can keep track of the changes I make as I go along. I've posted about this on my social media before and people seem to like getting this insight into my process. So, I've decided that these buns should be named 'Take 12' because, honestly, few things have ever taken me this long to perfect and this genuinely happened on the twelfth attempt! These buns were a big challenge and were something I never thought I would be able to make gluten free. They're pillowy soft, incredibly satisfying and I've filled them with a juicy pork filling that mimics the flavours and textures of char siu without having to go to the trouble of separately roasting pork.

**For the dough**
110 ml (3¾ fl oz) warm water (37–40°C/100–105°F is ideal)
100 ml (3½ fl oz) warm milk (37–40°C/100–105°F is ideal)
1 tablespoon instant dried yeast
2 tablespoons caster (superfine) sugar
260 g (9 oz) **basic flour blend** (page 18)
40 g (1½ oz) rice flour, plus extra for dusting
2½ teaspoons psyllium husk powder
2 teaspoons xanthan gum
4½ teaspoons gluten-free baking powder
½ teaspoon salt
70 g (2½ oz) egg whites
1 tablespoon vegetable oil, plus extra for greasing

**For the filling**
350 g (12½ oz) pork belly, cut into 2–3 cm (¾–1¼ in) cubes
2 tablespoons caster (superfine) sugar
¼ teaspoon salt
¼ teaspoon cracked black pepper
¾ teaspoon Chinese five spice
2 teaspoons gluten-free cornflour (cornstarch)
1 tablespoon vegetable oil
2 shallots, finely chopped
3 garlic cloves, minced
2 tablespoons gluten-free soy sauce
1 tablespoon sesame oil
1 tablespoon gluten-free oyster sauce
½ teaspoon rice vinegar
1 tablespoon gluten-free Shaoxing rice wine (or other cooking wine)
125 ml (4¼ fl oz) water

Start by making the dough. Add the water and milk to a medium jug or bowl, then mix in the yeast and 1 tablespoon of the sugar. Cover and leave in a warm, draft-free place for 10 minutes until the yeast has 'bloomed', which means there is a thick layer of foam on the surface. (If a layer of foam has not formed, your yeast may not be active and the buns will not work properly. See page 36 for guidance on working with yeast.)

In a mixing bowl or the bowl of a stand mixer, combine the rest of the dry ingredients, including the remaining 1 tablespoon of sugar, and make a well in the centre.

Whisk the egg whites into the water-milk-yeast mixture, then pour this into the dry ingredients. Mix vigorously with a wooden spoon or with a paddle beater on medium speed for 3–4 minutes, stopping regularly to scrape the side of the bowl.

*…continues overleaf*

Bring the dough together into a ball, then add the vegetable oil and mix for a further 3–4 minutes until the oil has been worked into the dough. It will be a sticky, wet dough at this stage.

Grease a clean bowl with a little vegetable oil, then use a spatula to gather and transfer the dough into the greased bowl. Shake and rotate the bowl a little to ensure the dough is a uniform ball, then flip it over. The aim is to have a smooth ball of dough that is greased all over. Cover loosely with cling film (plastic wrap), then a tea towel (dish towel), and place it in a warm, draft-free place to prove for 1 hour until doubled in size.

While the dough is proving, make the filling. Place the pork belly pieces in a bowl along with the sugar, salt, pepper, Chinese five spice and cornflour, then massage these seasonings into the meat with your hands.

Add the vegetable oil to a medium frying pan (skillet) and set over medium heat. When hot, add the pork belly and fry for 8–10 minutes, stirring very occasionally so that the meat gets a chance to caramelise.

When the pork belly pieces have browned and are starting to develop a crust, add the shallots and garlic to the pan. Stir fry until softened, then add the soy sauce, sesame oil, oyster sauce, rice vinegar and Shaoxing rice wine. Mix well, then add the water and allow to cook for 5–10 minutes, stirring occasionally, until most of the water has evaporated, leaving a thickened, rich sauce. Transfer the mixture to a plate to cool. Once it has cooled, roughly chop the pork into smaller pieces, then set aside.

Dust a clean work surface with rice flour and tip out the proved dough. Knead it vigorously for 2–3 minutes until smooth, only dusting with rice flour as absolutely necessary to prevent it sticking. Once smooth, roll the dough into a thick, 30 cm (11¾ in) log, then divide it into 6 even pieces.

Working with one piece at a time, roll the dough between your palms to form a smooth ball, then use a rolling pin to roll it into a disc about 1 cm (½ in) thick. Trying not to touch the 3–4 cm (1¼–1½ in) of dough in the centre, work the rolling pin outwards around the edge of the disc until it's about 15 cm (6 in) in diameter. It should be thicker in the middle than it is at the edges.

Place a small spoonful of the pork filling into the middle of the circle of dough, then bring the edges together on top of the filling, pleating as you go to seal the meat inside. Make sure the bun is completely sealed, then turn it over so that the sealed side is on the bottom. Neaten the bun by cupping your hands over it and rotating it gently. Place the finished bun, sealed side-down, on a square of baking paper that's slightly larger than the bun, then set it aside and repeat with the rest of the dough and filling.

Place the finished buns into stackable bamboo steamer baskets, spaced 3–4 cm (1¼ × 1½ in) apart. Stack the baskets, place the lid on, and leave to prove in a warm, draft-free place for 10 minutes. While they're proving, prepare a wok or pot for steaming – ensure that there is enough water to simmer under the baskets but not so much that any liquid will touch the buns.

Transfer the steamer baskets to the wok or pot and steam over medium heat for 12 minutes. Turn the heat off but leave the baskets in place with the lid on for 15–20 minutes (do not remove the lid before this as a dramatic change in temperature will cause the buns to collapse!). The buns will then be ready to serve.

# YOUTIAO
# (FRIED CHINESE DOUGH)

Makes 8

Youtiao are one of those foods that I never thought I would get to try. I didn't have them prior to my coeliac disease diagnosis and I'd never seen a gluten-free version until I created my own. I share this recipe having made them for plenty of gluten-eating friends who *have* had youtiao before and who have given them their tick of approval. They're crisp but chewy, and they hollow out and puff up beautifully! These are served as part of a dim sum spread as a 'bready' component, but can also be used as a topping for congee or as a filling in cheung fun (page 62).

100 g (3½ oz) warm water (37–40°C/100–105°F is ideal)
1 teaspoon instant dried yeast
1 teaspoon caster (superfine) sugar
120 g (4¼ oz) **basic flour blend** (page 18), plus extra for dusting
1½ teaspoons psyllium husk powder
½ teaspoon xanthan gum
1 teaspoon gluten-free baking powder
¼ teaspoon salt
40 g (1½ oz) egg, beaten
2 teaspoons vegetable oil, plus extra for greasing and deep-frying

NOTE

*This dough requires proving – for detailed instructions on working with yeasted dough or for troubleshooting help, see page 36.*

Add the water to a medium jug (pitcher) or bowl, then mix in the yeast and sugar. Cover and leave in a warm, draft-free place for 10 minutes until the yeast has 'bloomed', which means there is a thick layer of foam on the surface. (If a layer of foam has not formed, your yeast may not be active and the youtiao will not work properly. See page 36 for guidance on working with yeast.)

Meanwhile, in a large mixing bowl or the bowl of a stand mixer, combine the rest of the dry ingredients and make a well in the centre.

Whisk the beaten egg into the water-yeast mixture, then pour this into the dry ingredients. Mix vigorously with a wooden spoon or with a paddle beater on medium speed for 3–4 minutes, stopping regularly to scrape the side of the bowl. Bring the dough together into a ball, then add the vegetable oil and mix for a further 3–4 minutes until the oil has been worked into the dough. It will be a very sticky, wet dough at this stage.

Grease a clean bowl with a little vegetable oil, then use a spatula to gather and transfer the dough into the greased bowl. Shake and rotate the bowl a little to ensure the dough is a uniform ball, then flip it over. The aim is to have a smooth ball of dough that is greased all over. Cover loosely with cling film (plastic wrap), then a tea towel (dish towel), and place it in a warm, draft-free place to prove for 1 hour until doubled in size.

Transfer the proved dough to a lightly floured work surface and knead until smooth, then roll it into a 50 × 14 cm (20 × 5½ in) rectangle. Cut the dough into 16 strips that are 14 cm (5½ in) long and about 3 cm (1¼ in) wide.

...continues overleaf

To create the youtiao shape, wet your finger with a little water and run it down the middle of one strip of dough, then place a second strip of dough directly on top. Use a chopstick to gently but firmly press down the centre of the length of the dough strips. The two strips of dough should now be fused together in the centre while the dough on either side of the pressed line will have bulged slightly. Repeat with the remaining dough strips. You should end up with 8 youtiao. Place them on a tray dusted with flour and cover very loosely with cling film (plastic wrap), then a tea towel (dish towel), and leave in a warm, draft-free place to prove for a 40 minutes.

When about 10 minutes of proving time remains, place 6–7 cm (2½ × 2¾ in) of oil in a large, deep pan and set over medium heat. Check the oil temperature – when you're ready to fry it should be hot enough that a wooden chopstick or wooden spoon sizzles when dipped into the oil.

Working in batches to avoid overcrowding the pan, carefully lower the youtiao into the hot oil and fry for 5–6 minutes until a deep golden brown. Throughout the first minute of cooking, you must agitate and turn each youtiao constantly to ensure it puffs evenly in all directions. Remove from the oil using a slotted spoon and place on a cooling rack lined with paper towel while you fry the rest. The youtiao are ready to serve immediately.

pictured on page 65

# CRISPY RED BEAN PANCAKES

Makes 6

If you haven't had red bean paste before, or if you're not familiar with beans in sweet recipes, you might find the concept of these pancakes a little strange. I grew up eating red bean paste in various desserts, so these pancakes are a firm favourite of mine. They're surprisingly quite savoury, like many Asian desserts (think matcha and black sesame flavoured treats), but if you drizzle condensed milk over these crispy pancakes, you can make them as sweet as you like!

70 g (2½ oz) **basic flour blend** (page 18)
70 g (2½ oz) rice flour
70 g (2½ oz) tapioca starch
¼ teaspoon salt
2 tablespoons caster (superfine) sugar
1 egg
430 ml (14½ fl oz) water
neutral oil, for frying
150 g (5½ oz) red bean paste
sweetened condensed milk, to serve (optional)

In a large mixing bowl, whisk together the dry ingredients, then add the egg and water, whisking well to combine. Strain the batter through a mesh sieve into a clean bowl to remove any lumps of flour.

Lightly grease a large non-stick frying pan (skillet) with a little of the oil and place it over medium heat. Wipe away any excess oil with a paper towel.

Pour about 125 ml (4¼ fl oz) of batter into the frying pan and immediately lift and tilt the pan, swirling the batter so that it coats the base of the frying pan in a thin, even layer, like a crêpe. Turn the heat down to medium–low and allow to cook for 45 seconds–1 minute until the top of the crêpe has set, indicating it is cooked through. The edges will likely start to pull away from the frying pan but, if not, use a thin spatula to pry the edge of the crêpe away from the pan (if it is not coming off the pan, you may need to cook it a little longer). Now carefully peel it out of the pan using your fingers and transfer it to a board or plate. Repeat with most of the remaining batter, leaving 2 teaspoons of batter in the bowl.

Working one crêpe at a time, place a large spoonful of red bean paste (about 25 g/1 oz) into the centre of a crêpe and very gently spread it into a square about one-quarter or one-third of the size of the crêpe. Fold over the edges of the crêpe to completely cover the paste, using some of the reserved batter as glue to seal it closed. You now have red bean pancakes!

Place 1 cm (½ in) of neutral oil in a deep frying pan (skillet) and set it over medium heat. Check the oil temperature – when you're ready to fry it should be hot enough that a wooden chopstick or wooden spoon sizzles when dipped into the oil. Cooking one at a time, place a pancake seam side-down into the oil, and fry until the underside is a deep golden brown. Carefully flip the pancake and fry until the other side is the same colour. It may puff up; in which case you can apply gentle pressure to flatten it. If there is lots of resistance, do not apply force as this will likely create a hole in the pancake that will make the final result oily.

Transfer to a plate lined with paper towels to absorb any excess oil while you cook the remaining pancakes.

Cut the pancakes into bite-sized squares while hot and serve drizzled with condensed milk, if you like!

NOTE

*For convenience, I use ready-made red bean paste, which is quite easy to find at Asian grocery stores. It is relatively simple to make yourself so, if you decide to go down this route, just look up one of the many gluten-free recipes online.*

# MANGO PANCAKES

Makes 6

**Although these are called pancakes, they're actually more like crêpes that are rolled around a piece of fresh mango and a hearty dollop of lightly sweetened vanilla whipped cream. They're a delicious treat to end a dim sum feast and super easy to make!**

70 g (2½ oz) **basic flour blend** (page 18)
70 g (2½ oz) rice flour
70 g (2½ oz) tapioca starch
¼ teaspoon salt
2 tablespoons caster (superfine) sugar
1 egg
430 ml (14½ fl oz) water
3–5 drops yellow food colouring
1–2 teaspoons vegetable oil
2 fresh mangoes
300 ml (10 fl oz) chilled whipping cream
½ teaspoon vanilla bean paste (or extract)
3 tablespoons icing (powdered) sugar

In a large mixing bowl, whisk together the flours, starch, salt and caster sugar, then add the egg and water, whisking well to combine. Add just enough food colouring to make the batter bright yellow. Strain the batter through a mesh sieve into a clean bowl to remove any lumps of flour.

Lightly grease a large non-stick frying pan (skillet) with a little oil and place it over medium heat. Wipe away any excess oil with paper towel.

Pour about 120 ml (4 fl oz) of batter into the frying pan and immediately lift and tilt the pan, swirling the batter so that it coats the base of the frying pan in a thin, even layer.

Turn the heat down to medium–low and allow the crêpe to cook for 45 seconds–1 minute until the top has just set, indicating it is cooked through. The edges will likely start to pull away from the frying pan but, if not, use a thin spatula to pry the edge of the crêpe away from the pan (if it is not coming off the pan, you may need to cook it a little longer). Now carefully peel it out of the pan using your fingers and transfer it to a board or plate. Repeat with most of the remaining batter, until you have 6 crêpes.

While the crêpes cool, prepare the mango. If you have a sharp potato peeler, you'll be able to use that to peel the mangoes. Otherwise, use a sharp knife to remove the skin, leaving as much flesh on the seed as possible. Cut the cheeks off each mango, then cut 3 of the cheeks in half lengthways so that each crêpe can be filled with a single large piece of mango (I eat the leftover cheek as a snack!).

Add the cream, vanilla and icing sugar to a mixing bowl and whisk with a hand-held electric beater or stand mixer until stiff peaks form.

Working with one crêpe at a time, place a generous dollop of the whipped cream towards the edge of a crêpe and spread it out to be roughly the size of the mango portions. Place a piece of mango onto the cream, then gently fold the lower edge of the crêpe over the cream and mango. Bring the sides of the crêpe over onto the part enveloping the cream and mango, then roll it the rest of the way like a burrito.

Now you have a mango pancake! Place it seam-side down onto a serving dish, then repeat with the remaining crêpes and filling. Serve immediately.

# TEA PARTY FEAST

At this point, the token orange and almond cake offered as the only gluten-free option at the local café has become a bit of a running joke within the gluten-free community. While having at least one option is pleasant, I think we all feel that our horizons can be a little broader, especially given how far our knowledge of gluten-free cooking has come in the last five to ten years! Anyway, *enough* of missing out on variety or of missing out altogether. For this feast, I've created a collection of sweet and savoury recipes that could make up an epic morning or afternoon tea feast (or which could, frankly, be enjoyed on many occasions beyond that, too!).

# SCONES

Makes 8–10

I've been working on these for a long time! I was torn between trying to recreate an Australian scone or a more English scone – a distinction I didn't realise existed until living in the UK. At home in Australia, scones are like a fluffy, tender bread bun, often made with only three ingredients: flour, lemonade and cream. In the UK, I've found that scones are denser and more crumbly, with a focus on butter and the pillowy layers within the dough. I think this recipe actually combines the best of both worlds. They're buttery but still light and fluffy, and they are mild-flavoured – perfect to pair with a slathering of jam and thick cream.

260 g (9 oz) **basic flour blend** (page 18), plus extra for dusting
2 teaspoons gluten-free baking powder
¼ teaspoon salt
3 tablespoons caster (superfine) sugar
200 g (7 oz) butter, chilled and cubed
2 eggs, beaten, plus extra for egg wash
60 ml (2 fl oz) lemonade
1 teaspoon vanilla bean paste (or extract)
**whipped lemon butter** (overleaf), to serve
**raspberry thyme compote** (overleaf), to serve

Preheat the oven to 190°C Fan (375°F Fan) and line a baking sheet with baking paper.

Sift the dry ingredients into a medium bowl and mix them briefly. Add the cubed butter, then use your fingers to rub the butter into the dry ingredients until the mixture resembles coarse breadcrumbs.

Create a well in the centre of the ingredients, then add the eggs, lemonade and vanilla and mix with a spatula until just combined. It will be a wetter, stickier dough than is typical for scones.

Dust your work surface liberally with flour and scoop the dough onto it. Dust the top of the dough with more flour, then use your hands to pat it down until it's about 3 cm (1¼ in) thick.

Dip a 4 cm (1½ in) round cookie cutter in flour, then cut circles out of the dough, transferring them to the lined baking sheet. Be sure to leave 5–6 cm (2–2½ in) between each one. After cutting out as many rounds as possible, gather the dough scraps, mix them together in the original bowl you used, and repeat the patting and cutting process.

Use a pastry brush to brush the tops of the scones with some beaten egg, then bake them in the centre of the oven for 28–30 minutes until they're golden brown and have doubled in size.

Serve warm with my whipped lemon butter and raspberry thyme compote (overleaf), or simply with cream and jam (jelly).

## WHIPPED LEMON BUTTER

Makes about 250 g (9 oz)

250 g (9 oz) good-quality, unsalted butter, at room-temperature
1 teaspoon vanilla bean paste (or extract)
2 teaspoons lemon zest
½ teaspoon flaky salt
1 teaspoon lemon juice
1 tablespoon icing (powdered) sugar

Use a hand-held electric beater or stand mixer to whip the butter for 3–4 minutes until very pale and creamy, then add the remaining ingredients. Beat for a further 2–3 minutes until light and fluffy, then transfer to a serving bowl. It will keep in an airtight container in the fridge for 1–2 weeks.

*pictured on page 89*

## RASPBERRY THYME COMPOTE

Makes about 300 g (10½ oz)

300 g (10½ oz) frozen raspberries
3 tablespoons caster (superfine) sugar
1 tablespoon lemon juice
1 tablespoon water
5–6 thyme sprigs

Add all ingredients (except the thyme) to a small saucepan and place over medium heat. Allow it to come to a simmer as the berries thaw and begin to break down. Add the thyme sprigs and reduce the compote until it thickens and is able to coat the back of a spoon.

Transfer the compote to a clean bowl and allow to cool, then remove the thyme sprigs. The compote can be served warm for a looser consistency or chilled for a jammier texture. It will keep in an airtight container in the fridge for 1–2 weeks.

*pictured on page 89*

# STRAWBERRY CUSTARD DANISHES

*Makes 6*

Being able to make these Danishes is still such a huge novelty! I used to make them with puff pastry until I perfected my yeasted croissant dough – now I will never go back. The buttery and airy laminated pastry is just so perfect with the creamy custard and fresh strawberries. Feel free to mix this recipe up a little – you can experiment with custard flavours and berry combinations, or even go for something like rhubarb if that's what has been missing from your life!

**Day One**
1 quantity of **croissant dough** (page 38)

**Day Two**
4 egg yolks
120 ml (4 fl oz) single (light) cream, plus 1 tablespoon extra for egg wash
180 ml (6 fl oz) milk
1 teaspoon vanilla bean paste (or extract)
2 tablespoons caster (superfine) sugar
2½ teaspoons gluten-free cornflour (cornstarch)
⅛ teaspoon salt
about 250 g (9 oz) strawberries, hulled and quartered
icing (powdered) sugar, for dusting

**Day One**

Follow all the Day One instructions for the croissants on page 38.

**Day Two**

Follow the Day Two instructions for the croissants on pages 39–40 until you have completed the 'final roll'.

## CUT AND SHAPE

Use a sharp knife to carefully trim away any rough dough edges, leaving you with a neat rectangle measuring about 26 × 38 cm (10¼ × 15 in). Cut the rectangular sheet of dough into 12 equal portions. Do this by making 3 horizontal cuts about 10 cm (4 in) apart, and 2 vertical cuts about 9 cm (3½ in) apart. Each Danish will be made using 2 pieces of dough.

Use a 7 cm (2¾ in) round cookie cutter to cut out circles from the centre of 6 of the dough pieces.

Whisk together 1 egg yolk with the 1 tablespoon of extra cream in a small bowl. Use a pastry brush to coat the borders of the 6 un-cut dough pieces with a light layer of egg wash, then carefully place each piece of dough with a round hole cut out onto an uncut piece, aligning the edges as best you can. Transfer the pastry to baking sheet lined with baking paper, ensuring they are spaced at least 6–7 cm (2½–2¾ in) apart.

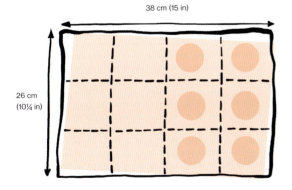

...continues overleaf

## PROVE AND PREP

Cover the pastry loosely with cling film (plastic wrap), then place in a warm, draft free place for 2–2.5 hours (see page 36 for proving tips).

While the pastry proves, make the filling. Add the cream, milk and vanilla to a medium saucepan and set over low heat, stirring regularly. Place the caster sugar, cornflour, salt and remaining 3 egg yolks into a mixing bowl and whisk vigorously until pale and creamy.

When the milk and cream mixture is just about to simmer, trickle it over the egg mixture, whisking constantly. Once fully combined, pour the mixture back into the saucepan and place over low heat, whisking constantly until the custard has thickened (and there is no floury taste). Transfer the custard to a clean bowl and cover with cling film (plastic wrap), ensuring the plastic is in contact with the surface of the custard (this will prevent a skin from forming). Allow to cool, then place in the fridge to chill completely.

When the pastry has about 20 minutes of proving time remaining, preheat the oven to 200°C Fan (400°F Fan).

## BAKE AND FILL

When the pastry has proved, each one will have grown about 75% in size. They should appear puffy, but not dimpled. If the pastries are dimpled, they may be overproved, which will affect their rise in the oven and the final texture, so keep a close eye on them (if they start to appear dimpled, end the proving period early).

Remove the cling film and use a pastry brush to gently brush the top and cut-out hole with egg wash. Apply the egg wash only to the uncut portions of dough; avoid the cut edges as much as possible as this can seal the layers closed, which will affect how the Danishes rise. When all Danishes have been coated in egg wash, transfer the baking sheet to the centre of your oven.

Bake the Danishes for 5 minutes, then reduce the oven temperature to 160°C Fan (325°F Fan). Cook for a further 25 minutes, then reduce the oven temperature to 140°C Fan (285°F Fan). Cook for a further 20–25 minutes, until the pastry is a rich golden brown, then remove them from the oven and allow them to cool fully on the baking sheet.

Whisk the chilled custard to loosen it, then transfer it to a piping bag. Dust the pastries with icing sugar, then fill them with a generous portion of the custard. Top with strawberries to finish, and the Danishes are ready to serve.

# SALMON AND DILL PROFITEROLES

*Makes about 12*

Choux pastry offers an excellent alternative to bread when it comes to a savoury treat; they're surprisingly easy to make and no-one will know that these are gluten free! I've opted to fill them with salmon and a herby homemade mayonnaise – if you have any filling leftover, try spreading it on crackers or sliced gluten-free bread for a delicious lunch.

350–400 g (12–14 oz) raw salmon fillets, deboned and skin removed
1 teaspoon extra virgin olive oil
salt and cracked black pepper

**For the choux pastry**
125 ml (4½ fl oz) water
55 g (2 oz) unsalted butter
60 g (2¼ oz) rice flour
100 g (3½ oz) eggs, beaten (about 2 eggs)

**For the herby mayonnaise**
1 egg
2 teaspoons Dijon mustard
1 teaspoon apple cider vinegar
1 tablespoon lemon juice
220 ml (7½ fl oz) vegetable oil
3 teaspoons wholegrain mustard
½ teaspoon honey
4 tablespoons finely chopped chives
3 tablespoons finely chopped dill
3 teaspoons capers, roughly chopped

Preheat the oven to 190°C Fan (375°F Fan) and line a large baking sheet with baking paper.

Start by making the choux pastry. Add the water, butter and ⅛ teaspoon of salt to a small saucepan and place it over medium heat. When the water is simmering and the butter has completely melted, reduce the temperature to low. Working quickly, add the rice flour and mix with a sturdy spatula to bring the mixture together as a dough. Continue mixing the dough over low heat for about 20 seconds, then transfer it to a large bowl or the bowl of your stand mixer (fitted with the whisk attachment).

Using a hand-held electric beater or stand mixer, immediately start mixing the dough on a medium-high speed. Trickle in the beaten eggs, mixing constantly and being careful not to pour too quickly (if the egg pools in the bowl it may get scrambled by the hot dough). Beat the dough until it is smooth and creamy, scraping down the side of the bowl as necessary, then transfer to a piping bag.

Pipe blobs of choux pastry onto the prepared baking sheet. Each one should be roughly 1 tablespoon of mixture but a little more or less is fine. Make sure you space them 3–4 cm (1¼–1½ in) apart so that they won't touch as they bake.

Bake for 30–35 minutes. When the choux have fully puffed and are golden brown all over, turn the oven off but leave the door ajar for a further 10–15 minutes. This will help them dry on the inside and prevent possible collapsing.

...continues overleaf

To make the mayonnaise, in the canister of a stick blender or a tall jug (pitcher), place the egg, ¼ teaspoon of salt, the Dijon mustard, vinegar, lemon juice and vegetable oil. Place the stick blender all the way into the canister (or jug) so it sits on the bottom, then blitz, without moving it, until the egg emulsifies with the oil. Now very slowly move the stick blender (while still blitzing) upwards through the rest of the ingredients until you have a homogenous, thick mayonnaise. (Alternatively, you can use a blender or food processor – to do so, start by mixing the above ingredients without the oil, then slowly trickle the oil in as you mix.) Stir in the wholegrain mustard, honey, herbs and capers, then set aside while you cook the salmon.

Drizzle the salmon fillets with the olive oil and season with salt and pepper. Either pan fry over medium heat for 7–8 minutes until just cooked through, or place on a lined baking tray and bake at 180°C Fan (350°F Fan) for 12–14 minutes. Allow to cool, then flake the cooked salmon into a mixing bowl. Add 4-5 tablespoons of the herbed mayonnaise (or more if you want it creamier) and mix until well combined, then season with more salt and pepper to taste.

To assemble, slice the choux pastry profiteroles in half horizontally – they should be almost entirely hollow (if not, pull out any excess dough from the centre). Spoon a generous portion of the salmon and mayo mixture into each of the profiteroles then replace the choux tops. Serve them immediately.

NOTE

*You can prep these ahead but the choux and filling will need to be stored separately. Store the choux in an airtight container at room temperature, but be aware that if there's any moisture in the container they will soften during storage (I usually make them in the morning on the day I want to serve them and simply set them to one side in my kitchen until I'm ready to fill them). Store the filling in a covered bowl in the fridge.*

*You will be left with a little extra herby mayonnaise. Store it in an airtight container in the fridge for up to 1 week. It's delicious in a potato salad or smeared on a bagel and topped with smoked salmon.*

# DOUBLE CHOCOLATE CHOUX PUFFS

Makes about 12

These choux puffs are a variation of the choux used on page 96, but they include what is called 'craquelin'. This is essentially a simple biscuit layer that is baked onto the choux pastry, creating a sweet, crunchy layer. It not only adds flavour and texture, but helps the choux to rise into perfectly round, uniform buns. I love to add this to my sweet choux pastries as those fillings are often so creamy that they really benefit from the texture of a slightly crunchy topping. These double chocolate choux are rich and luxurious, with two types of chocolate filling to balance out the sweetness and complement the other, generally lighter flavours found in this feast.

1 quantity of **choux pastry** (page 96)
icing (powdered) sugar, for dusting

**For the chocolate crème pâtissiere**
200 ml (6¾ fl oz) single (light) cream
300 ml (10 fl oz) milk
2 teaspoons vanilla bean paste (or extract)
4 eggs
75 g (2¾ oz) caster (superfine) sugar
40 g (1½ oz) gluten-free cornflour (cornstarch)
⅛ teaspoon salt
150 g (5¼ oz) dark (bittersweet) chocolate, chopped

**For the craquelin**
45 g (1½ oz) unsalted butter, at room temperature
50 g (1¾ oz) caster (superfine) sugar
40 g (1½ oz) **basic flour blend** (page 18)
10 g (⅓ oz) unsweetened cocoa powder

**For the dark chocolate ganache**
50 g (1¾ oz) dark (bittersweet) chocolate, chopped
2 tablespoons single (light) cream

Start by making the chocolate crème pâtissiere. Add the milk, cream and vanilla to a medium saucepan and set it over low heat, stirring regularly. Meanwhile, place the eggs, caster sugar, cornflour and salt in a mixing bowl and whisk vigorously until smooth and creamy. Place the chopped chocolate in a separate mixing bowl and set aside.

When the milk is just about to simmer, trickle it over the egg mixture, whisking constantly. Once fully combined, pour the mixture back into the saucepan and place over low heat, whisking constantly for 2–3 minutes until the crème pâtissiere has thickened considerably (and there is no floury taste). Transfer the crème pâtissiere to the bowl with the chocolate and allow it to sit for 1–2 minutes, before stirring until completely combined and even in colour. Cover with cling film (plastic wrap), ensuring the plastic is in contact with the surface of the crème pâtissiere (this will prevent a skin from forming). Allow to cool, then place in the fridge to chill completely.

Now prepare the craquelin. Combine the butter and caster sugar in a small bowl and mix well, then stir in the flour and cocoa powder until it forms a smooth dough. Place the dough between two large sheets of baking paper, then flatten it with your hands. Use a rolling pin to roll the dough out into a thin layer, about 3–4 mm (⅛ in) thick. Keeping it within the baking paper sheets, transfer it to a baking sheet or chopping board and place it in the freezer. Keep it as flat as possible to make cutting easier later.

Preheat the oven to 190°C Fan (375°F Fan) and line a large baking sheet with baking paper.

...continues overleaf

Make the choux pastry according to the instructions on page 96 and transfer it to a piping bag, then pipe blobs of choux pastry onto the prepared baking sheet. Each one should be roughly 1 tablespoon of mixture but a little more or less is fine. Make sure you space them 3–4 cm (1¼–1½ in) apart so that they won't touch as they bake.

Remove the craquelin from the freezer and, using a cookie cutter that is slightly larger than the circumference of the choux pastry blobs, cut rounds out of the craquelin dough and place them gently on top of each choux pastry blob.

Bake the choux pastry for 30–35 minutes. When the choux pastries have fully puffed and are golden brown all over, turn the oven off but leave the door ajar for a further 10–15 minutes. This will help them dry on the inside and prevent possible collapsing.

When the choux have cooled and the chocolate crème pâtissiere has fully chilled, make the dark chocolate ganache. Place the chocolate in a microwave-safe bowl, add the cream and microwave on high (900W) for 30 seconds. Stir to combine, then microwave for a further 15–30 seconds if necessary to make the ganache smooth (you can also do this in a small saucepan – simply stir the ingredients over low heat until melted and combined). Set aside to cool while you start filling the choux.

Use a small, serrated knife to pierce the base of each choux pastry twice in an 'X' formation. This will allow you to fill the choux without cutting them in half, although you can simply halve them if you prefer and spoon or pipe in the two fillings.

Transfer the chilled chocolate crème pâtissiere to a piping bag, cut a 1 cm (½ in) hole in the end, and push the tip through the pierced hole to fill each choux pastry.

Transfer the cooled chocolate ganache to another piping bag, cut a 0.5 cm (¼ in) hole in the end, then pipe a small amount (about half a teaspoon) into each puff. If a little chocolate crème pâtissiere oozes out around the piping bag, that's fine, you can easily wipe it away afterwards.

Each puff should now be filled with chocolate crème pâtissiere with a rich, ganache centre. Dust the choux puffs with a little icing sugar, then serve.

# CRÈME BRÛLÉE TART

Serves 8

This is a new favourite dessert of mine because it's relatively simple to make but utterly delicious. It's also versatile! Although I brûlée the top, you can easily opt to top the tart with a dusting of cinnamon and nutmeg instead to make a nostalgic custard tart (just like the typical Aussie bakery ones I *loved* as a kid!).

### For the sweet pastry
- 115 g (4 oz) caster (superfine) sugar
- 60 g (2 oz) butter, chilled and cubed
- 25 g (1 oz) egg, beaten (about ½ a large egg)
- ½ teaspoon vanilla bean paste (or extract)
- 150 g (5¼ oz) **basic flour blend** (page 18), plus extra for dusting
- ½ teaspoon xanthan gum
- ⅛ teaspoon salt
- 1 tablespoon milk (if needed)
- 1 egg white
- 2 tablespoons single (light) cream

### For the custard filling
- 320 ml (11 fl oz) double (heavy) cream
- 2 teaspoons vanilla bean paste (or extract)
- 4 egg yolks
- 45 g (1½ oz) caster (superfine) sugar
- ⅛ teaspoon salt

### For the brûlée
- 6–8 teaspoons caster (superfine) sugar

Start by making the pastry. Preheat the oven to 160°C Fan (325°F Fan) and grease an 18–20 cm (7–8 in) fluted tart tin.

Cream the sugar and butter in a large bowl with a hand-held electric beater or in a stand mixer fitted with a whisk attachment. Add the egg and vanilla and continue mixing until well combined.

Sift together the dry ingredients, then add them to the egg and butter mixture. If using a stand mixer, mix a little by hand (to avoid blowing the flour out of the bowl), then switch to a paddle attachment and mix on medium speed until soft and smooth (this will take a few minutes). If mixing by hand, bring the dough together with a sturdy spatula, then knead it by hand until smooth and pliable. If needed, add a little of the milk – just enough for the dough to be soft and workable. Wrap the dough loosely in cling film (plastic wrap) and squash it into a thin disc. Refrigerate for 10–15 minutes.

Lightly dust your work surface with flour and remove the dough from the plastic. Dust the dough as well, then use a rolling pin to roll it out until it's 2–3 mm (1/16–1/8 in) thick.

Carefully transfer the pastry to the tart tin, gently pressing it to the base and edges before cutting away the excess pastry. Prick the base of the tart case all over with a fork, then place on a baking sheet and transfer to the oven for 16–18 minutes.

...continues overleaf

Beat together the egg white and single cream in a small bowl. Briefly remove the tart shell from the oven and use a pastry brush to coat the inside with a layer of egg wash. Place back in the oven to cook for a further 28–30 minutes until the pastry is a light golden brown.

Meanwhile, make the custard filling. Heat the double cream and vanilla in a medium saucepan over low heat, stirring regularly. In another bowl, whisk together the egg yolks, sugar and salt until pale and creamy. When the cream is just about to simmer, remove from the heat and trickle over the egg yolk mixture, whisking constantly. Strain the custard through a sieve into a pouring jug (pitcher) to remove any lumps.

When the tart shell is ready, turn the oven down to 130°C Fan (275°F Fan) and open the oven door. Slide the tart case out of the oven very slightly and carefully pour the custard into the tart shell. Doing this helps to reduce the oven temperature quickly and reduces the risk of the custard spilling out of the shell. Fill the pastry to the brim, then very carefully slide the tart back into the oven and close the door. Cook for a further 36–38 minutes.

When cooked, the custard will be set around the edges but still have a slight wobble in the centre. Remove it from the oven but allow to cool in the tart tin for 30–40 minutes, then transfer it to the fridge for 3–4 hours to chill completely. If you have a loose bottom tin, you should be able to remove the tart from the tin at this point but if not, it will be easier if you wait until the tart has completely chilled.

Slice the tart into 8 equal slices with a sharp, warm knife, cleaning it after each cut to maintain neat slices. When ready to serve, brûlée one slice at a time. Place a slice onto a baking sheet and sprinkle ½–1 teaspoon of the sugar in an even layer over the surface of the custard. Use a brûlée torch to caramelise the sugar on top of the tart, being careful not to burn the pastry. You should do this as quickly as possible to prevent the heat of the torch affecting the texture of the custard. Allow the caramelised sugar to harden for about 1 minute, then serve immediately.

NOTE

*If you don't want to brûlée your tart (see intro), simply combine ½ teaspoon of ground cinnamon with ½ teaspoon of ground nutmeg, then use a fine mesh sieve to dust this over the tart after baking.*

# BLUEBERRY FRANGIPANE TARTLETS

*Makes 12*

**These are delicious little pastries, perfect for any sort of morning tea or even dessert. You can also use this recipe to make a single, larger tart (just bake for an extra 5 minutes to ensure the filling is cooked through).**

90 g (3¼ oz) caster (superfine) sugar
90 g (3¼ oz) unsalted butter, at room-temperature
75 g (2¾ oz) egg, beaten (about 1½ large eggs)
1½ teaspoons vanilla bean paste (or extract)
90 g (3¼ oz) ground almonds
2 teaspoons **basic flour blend** (page 18)
⅓ teaspoon gluten-free baking powder
¼ teaspoon salt
70 g (2½ oz) fresh blueberries

**For the pastry**
115 g (4 oz) caster (superfine) sugar
60 g (2 oz) butter, chilled and cubed
25 g (1 oz) egg, beaten (about ½ a large egg)
½ teaspoon vanilla bean paste (or extract)
150 g (5¼ oz) **basic flour blend** (page 18), plus extra for dusting
½ teaspoon xanthan gum
⅛ teaspoon salt
1 tablespoon milk (if needed)

Start by making the pastry. Preheat the oven to 160°C Fan (325°F Fan) and grease 12 small, fluted tart tins. You can also use a muffin tray (if so, I recommend greasing the muffins holes and lining each base with a circle of baking paper, to ensure easy removal).

In a large bowl, cream the sugar and butter with a hand-held electric beater or stand mixer fitted with a whisk attachment. Add the egg and vanilla and continue mixing until combined.

Sift together the dry ingredients, then add them to the egg and butter mixture. If using a stand mixer, mix a little by hand (to avoid blowing the flour out of the bowl), then switch to a paddle attachment and mix on medium speed until soft and smooth (this will take a few minutes). If mixing by hand, bring the dough together with a sturdy spatula, then knead it by hand until smooth and pliable. If needed, add a little of the milk – just enough for the dough to be soft and workable. Wrap the dough loosely in cling film (plastic wrap) and squash it into a thin disc. Refrigerate for 10–15 minutes.

Lightly dust your work surface with flour and remove the dough from the plastic. Dust the dough as well, then use a rolling pin to roll it out until it's 2–3 mm (1/16–⅛ in) thick. Use a 4 cm (1½ in) round cookie cutter (it should be wider than the width of the tart tins) to cut out 12 circles of pastry.

Press the pastry into the tart tins (or muffin tray) and prick the bases generously with a fork. Place the tart tins on a baking sheet and transfer it the oven for 10–12 minutes.

While the tart cases are baking, make the filling. In a medium bowl, whisk together the sugar, butter, egg and vanilla until pale and slightly fluffy. Add the remaining ingredients (except the blueberries) and mix well to combine.

Remove the pastry cases from the oven and spoon some filling into each one until they are half full. Place 3 or 4 blueberries into each one, pressing them gently into the filling mixture.

Transfer them back to the oven and bake for a further 25–30 minutes until the tarts are golden brown. Allow to cool in the tart tins for 15–20 minutes before removing them and transferring to a cooling rack. They can be served warm or cool. If storing, allow to cool completely before sealing in an airtight container and placing in the fridge for up to 6 days.

# PUFF PASTRY
# (THE ULTIMATE SAVOURY PASTRY)

Makes 6–8

I've made many versions of savoury pastries for tarts or pies, but I was never completely happy with either the taste or texture, until I perfected *this* recipe! It is very versatile, making a wonderful puff pastry with crisp but delicate buttery layers, but it can also be adjusted to be a sort of puff-shortcrust hybrid. This requires no other ingredients, just a small extra step in the lamination process – that is, the way that the butter is folded into the dough to create layers. The shortcrust created has all the buttery delicacy of puff but it's more structurally sound, making it *perfect* for savoury tart or pie bases. The best part? It's delicious, requires no blind baking, and it's never soggy. I've tested it on my gluten-eating friends and it is always a hit, so I'm sure you're going to love it!

240 g (8½ oz) unsalted butter, chilled
150 g (5¼ oz) **basic flour blend** (page 18), plus extra for dusting
½ teaspoon caster (superfine) sugar
¼ teaspoon salt
½ teaspoon xanthan gum
¾ teaspoon gluten-free baking powder
½ teaspoon psyllium husk powder
4½ tablespoons water, chilled

## TO PREP THE BUTTER

Halve the chilled block of butter into 2 equal portions of 120 g (4¼ oz). Cut half into cubes and leave the other half in as compact a block as possible. Place both portions of butter on a plate and into the freezer (the plate will be of use later).

## TO MAKE THE DOUGH

Add the remaining ingredients (except the water) to the bowl of a food processor or stand mixer. Combine briefly, then add the cubed butter and mix again until the texture resembles very coarse breadcrumbs. With the mixer still running vigorously, trickle in the chilled water. The dough should start to clump and begin cleaning the side of the bowl. It will be a wetter dough than you might expect, with moist crumbs that can easily be pressed together with your fingers.

Tip the dough onto a sheet of cling film (plastic wrap) and fold it over and around the pastry. Use a rolling pin to flatten, squash and roll the pastry inside the cling film into a 20 cm (8 in) square. Don't be afraid to apply some pressure and stretch the plastic and bring the dough into shape. Refrigerate for 10 minutes, keeping it as flat as possible.

Meanwhile, remove the second block of butter and plate from the freezer and, working as quickly as possible, grate the butter into an even layer onto the cold plate. Place the grated butter back into the freezer.

Prepare a large sheet of baking paper on your work surface. Generously dust the parchment with flour, then unwrap the chilled pastry and place it in the centre of the baking paper, dusting the pastry with flour, too.

Use a large rolling pin to roll the pastry out into a rectangular shape, moving the dough around on the paper regularly as you do so and adding a little flour as necessary. When it measures about 22 × 36 cm (8¾ × 14 in), position the pastry so that a short edge is closest to you. Use a dry pastry brush to quickly brush away all excess flour from the surface of the dough. Use a knife to very gentle score the dough into 3 equal sections, so you have a bottom, centre and top section – this is just to mark the dough, not to cut all the way through.

Working as quickly as possible, spread half the chilled, grated butter over the centre third of the dough. When you have an even a layer as possible, apply some pressure with your hands to compress the butter gently into the dough (this attaches it to the dough but also allows some of the warmth from your hands to soften any sharp pieces of butter, preventing them from piercing the dough). Take the bottom third of dough (the one closest to you) and fold it up and over the centre third. Do not try to stretch the corners to align perfectly, but make it fit as best you can. Use the pastry brush to dust away any excess flour on the newly exposed surface, then press the dough gently down onto the butter.

Spread the second half of the chilled, grated butter over the newly exposed layer of pastry, again spreading it as evenly as possible. Gently press it down with your hands, then bring the remaining top third of dough (the one furthest away from you) over the butter layer, aligning the edges as neatly as possible without breaking the dough. Compress the dough gently onto the butter with your fingers.

Rotate the dough 90 degrees so that a short edge is once again closest to you, then flour the baking paper and dough once more. Use your rolling pin to make lots of small lengthways dents over the dough, then begin to roll it out again, moving the dough around the baking paper as you do so, and dusting with flour as needed.

...continues overleaf

Roll it out into a rectangle, again measuring about 22 × 36 cm (8¾ × 14 in), then brush away any excess flour from the surface of the dough. Once again, fold the lower third up and over the centre third, brush away the excess flour, then fold the top third over the newly exposed dough, aligning the edges as neatly as possible. Compress gently so the dough remains in place.

## FOR PUFF PASTRY

Once again, rotate the dough 90 degrees so that a short edge is closest to you, then roll it out into a rectangle, again measuring about 22 × 36 cm (8¾ × 14 in). At this point, you have puff pastry! Transfer it to a chopping board, cover it with cling film and refrigerate for at least 20 minutes, or until you're ready to use it.

## FOR A PUFF-SHORTCRUST HYBRID PASTRY

If you're making pastry for the base of a pie, tart or quiche that needs more of a buttery crumb, rather than flaky layers (see intro on page 106), follow the instructions above for the puff pastry, then complete one more set of folding and rolling. Transfer it to a chopping board, cover it with cling film and refrigerate for at least 20 minutes, or until you're ready to use it.

## NOTES

*Freezing the butter isn't something you need to do beforehand; I've included it as the first step in the recipe, which should make it an ideal temperature and texture for when you need to use it. This does require the butter to be fridge-cold prior to starting though, so make sure you store it in the fridge for some time before starting this recipe.*

*This dough should be kept reasonably cold while you work with it, which means you'll have to use your judgment based on the temperature of your kitchen. You may need to refrigerate between folds if the dough is feeling warm or a little greasy – this means that the butter is softening too quickly.*

*If using this pastry recipe for any savoury pies, tarts or quiches not featured in this book, do note that the cook time is generally about 35 minutes at 180°C (350°F), so account for that if using the pastry with your own fillings.*

# CARAMELISED ONION, MUSHROOM AND BRIE TARTLETS

Makes 12

**These little morsels are an excellent way to enjoy my perfected savoury pastry (page 106) because the buttery dough goes so beautifully with the filling of slightly sweet onions and rich, fragrant mushrooms.**

1 quantity of **puff-shortcrust hybrid pastry** (page 106)
1½ tablespoons unsalted butter, plus extra for greasing
2 tablespoons extra virgin olive oil
3 onions, sliced
250 g (9 oz) button mushrooms, sliced
3–4 thyme sprigs, leaves picked
3 eggs
1½ tablespoons single (light) cream
150 g (5½ oz) Brie, sliced
a few chives, finely chopped, to serve (optional)
salt and cracked black pepper

Prepare the puff-shortcrust hybrid pastry according to the instructions on page 106.

Grease 12 small, fluted tart tins with butter. You can also use a muffin tray (if so, I recommend greasing the muffins holes and lining each muffin hole base with a circle of baking paper, to ensure easy removal of the pastry).

Use a 4 cm (1½ in) round cookie cutter (it should be wider than the width of the tart tins) to cut out 12 circles of pastry. Press the pastry into the tart tins (or muffin tray) and prick the bases 2–3 times with a fork. Place the tart tins on a baking sheet and refrigerate while you prep the filling.

Preheat the oven to 180°C Fan (350°F Fan).

Add the butter, oil, onions and ½ teaspoon of salt to a frying pan (skillet) set over medium heat. Stir regularly for 6–8 minutes, until the onions are softened and translucent, then add the mushrooms and thyme leaves. Cook for 10–15 minutes, stirring occasionally, so the onions and mushrooms brown and caramelise (but don't burn).

Meanwhile, beat the eggs in a jug (pitcher) with the cream and plenty of salt and pepper.

Divide the onion and mushroom mixture between the pastry cases, then pour some of the egg on top until the pastry cases are three-quarters full. Use a fork to move the filling around a bit to ensure the egg is dispersed through the onion and mushroom mixture.

Top each tart with 1–2 slices of the Brie, then transfer the tarts (still on the baking sheet) to the oven. Bake for 35 minutes, rotating once throughout the cook time if they seem to be browning unevenly.

Allow the tartlets to cool in the tart tins for 10–15 minutes before removing them and transferring to a cooling rack. Garnish with chopped chives and serve warm, or allow to cool completely before storing in an airtight container in the fridge for up to 4 days.

NOTE

*Any leftover pastry can be gathered and rerolled, or wrapped in cling film (plastic wrap), then stored in the fridge for another time (or simply make a bigger batch of tarts!).*

# PICNIC FEAST

Picnics are a great way to enjoy food with friends or family, and I feel like there's something about eating outdoors that somehow makes food taste even better. As with any other outings where food is shared though, this undoubtedly comes with some level of discomfort and anxiety for gluten-free people – either because of the concern that others won't like their food, or their worry about eating food prepared by someone else. My solution is to make food that is delicious and can be enjoyed by everyone, meaning that you get to participate in the sharing while also staying safe and having plenty to eat! This collection of recipes includes savoury and sweet options, all of which are easily packed for travel and perfect to be portioned out and eaten by hand.

# CHEDDAR AND ROSEMARY CRACKERS

Serves 3–4

Funnily enough, these crackers came about as a bit of a fluke when I was working to perfect my puff pastry (page 106). I was experimenting with the idea of a cheese-based pastry and although I ended up preferring the full butter version for a more versatile puff, I loved the cheesy one so much that I figured I'd convert it into some delicious crackers. These are crisp, a little flaky and very tasty, especially when topped with some extra cheese or dunked into your favourite dip (try my chunky romesco sauce on page overleaf!).

100 g (3½ oz) **basic flour blend** (page 18), plus extra for dusting
¼ teaspoon xanthan gum
½ teaspoon gluten-free baking powder
¼ teaspoon psyllium husk powder
⅛ teaspoon salt
¼ teaspoon caster (superfine) sugar
⅛ teaspoon garlic powder
1–2 rosemary sprigs, leaves picked and roughly chopped
50 g (1¾ oz) unsalted butter, chilled and cubed
75 g (2¾ oz) mature Cheddar, chilled and chilled
3 tablespoons water, chilled

Add all the dry ingredients to the bowl of a food processor and pulse to combine.

Add the butter and Cheddar and pulse until crumbly, then trickle in the chilled water as you mix on a medium speed. The dough should start to clump and begin cleaning the side of the bowl. It should still be crumbly at this stage but not floury.

Tip the dough onto a sheet of cling film (plastic wrap) and fold it over and around the pastry. Use a rolling pin to flatten, squash and roll the pastry inside the cling film into a 15 cm (6 in) square. Don't be afraid to apply some pressure and stretch the plastic to bring the dough into shape. Refrigerate for 20 minutes.

Dust your work surface with flour, then unwrap the chilled pastry and place it on the surface, dusting it with flour, too. Use a large rolling pin to roll the pastry out into a rectangle about 5 mm (¼ in) thick, moving the dough around regularly as you do so and adding a little flour as necessary. Use a dry pastry brush to quickly brush away all excess flour from the surface of the dough. Fold the bottom third of dough over the centre third, brush away any excess flour, then fold the top third over the newly exposed dough. Roll this out just a little, then wrap with cling film again and refrigerate for another 20 minutes.

Preheat the oven to 180°C Fan (350°F Fan) and line a baking sheet with baking paper.

Roll out the dough again, this time to 2–3 mm (¹⁄₁₆–⅛ in) thick, then use a sharp knife to cut it into cracker shapes. I usually cut mine into 4 cm (1½ in) squares, but you can make them rectangular and/or use a fluted pasta/pastry cutter to create wavy edges, or simply use a cookie cutter to cut them out.

Transfer them to the baking sheet, evenly spaced, then prick each cracker 2–3 times with a fork. Bake for 26–28 minutes until they're golden brown.

Allow to cool on the baking sheet, then eat them warm or cold. Allow to cool completely before storing in an airtight container.

# CHUNKY ROMESCO SAUCE

Serves 3–4

This sauce is great as a dip for my Cheddar and rosemary crackers (page 114), but it's also delicious in sandwiches (especially cheese toasties) or used as a creamy base for a veggie side dish – try topping it with roasted aubergine (eggplant), crumbled feta, chopped parsley and a squeeze of lemon.

1 large tomato, halved
2 red (bell) peppers, halved and deseeded
1 whole garlic bulb
extra virgin olive oil, for drizzling
75 g (2¾ oz) cashew nuts
1 slice of gluten-free bread, torn
1½ tablespoons sherry vinegar
1 tablespoon smoked paprika
1 teaspoon salt

Preheat the oven to 220°C Fan (425°F Fan) and line an roasting tray with baking paper. Place the tomato and red pepper cut side-down on the tray.

Slice the top off the garlic bulb and place it on a sheet of foil. Drizzle the garlic bulb with 1 teaspoon of olive oil, then wrap it up in the foil and place it on the tray with the vegetables. Roast for 25–30 minutes, or until the pepper skins are lightly charred.

While the vegetables are cooking, lightly toast the cashews in a frying pan (skillet) set over medium heat, then set aside. They should be fragrant and a little crunchy, but not brown.

Allow the vegetables to cool until cool enough to handle, then peel away the skin from the tomato and peppers – there's no need to be precise with this, just remove any loose or charred pieces. Place the tomato and pepper in the bowl of a food processor or blender. Unwrap the garlic and squeeze the flesh of the cloves into the processor, too.

Add all the remaining ingredients, along with 2 tablespoon of olive oil, to the processor and blitz to your preferred consistency (a little chunky or completely smooth). Transfer to a serving dish or sealable container.

# SUMMER VEGETABLE TART

Serves 6–8

This tart is a great option to slice and share at a picnic, especially if you want something a little fancier than sandwiches or rolls. There is heaps of flavour from the garlicky and herby courgettes – their sweetness goes beautifully with the tangy goats cheese on top.

1 quantity of **puff-shortcrust hybrid pastry** (page 106)
2 tablespoons extra virgin olive oil, plus extra for greasing
3–4 garlic cloves, minced
1 red chilli, deseeded and finely chopped
2–3 courgettes (zucchini) (about 600–700 g/ 21–25 oz total weight), finely sliced
2 tablespoons finely chopped parsley
2 tablespoons finely chopped basil
10–12 asparagus spears, trimmed
9 eggs
70 ml (2½ fl oz) single (light) cream
100 g (3½ oz) soft goats cheese
flaky salt and cracked black pepper

Preheat the oven to 180°C Fan (350°F Fan) and grease a 26 cm (10 in) pie or tart tin with oil.

Roll out the pastry according to the directions on page 109, then drape it over the tart tin. Press the pastry gently into the base and sides of the tin before using a small, sharp knife to trim away any overhanging pastry. Use a fork to prick holes around the base of the pastry case, then line it with baking paper and fill with baking beans (pie weights).

Bake for 30 minutes, then remove the baking beans and parchment. If the base of the pastry is still soft, cook uncovered for another 10 minutes.

While the pastry is baking, prepare the filling. Add the oil, garlic and chilli to a large frying pan (skillet) set over medium heat and fry, stirring regularly, for 3–4 minutes until fragrant. Add the courgettes, along with 1 teaspoon of flaky salt, and cook for 12–14 minutes, stirring regularly, until the courgettes have softened significantly and started to caramelise. They should have reduced in volume by 60–70%. Add the herbs and stir to combine, then remove from the heat. Season with more salt to taste.

Spread the courgette mixture around the base of the pastry case in an even layer, then arrange the asparagus on top, trimming where necessary to make them fit in an even layer.

Whisk together the eggs, cream and some salt and pepper in a mixing bowl until combined, then pour this evenly over the vegetables in the pastry case. Use your fingers to crumble the goats cheese over the top of the tart.

Bake the tart for 30–35 minutes, until the filling is cooked through and the pastry is crisp. Allow to cool in the tin for at least 30 minutes before removing and placing on a cooling rack or board for slicing. This tart can be served hot or cold.

# SANDWICH LOAF (OR ROLLS)

Makes 1 large loaf
(or 8–12 rolls)

This bread was a major breakthrough and I'm so excited to share it. It's a bread that cooks beautifully in a loaf tin, but which also works really well for rolls and hot dog buns – like my prawn rolls (page 140). The crust is softer than the rustic loaves from my first book, which makes it great for lunch box sandwiches and rolls. It's soft and slightly buttery, without being too rich or sweet – just like a 'normal' white sandwich loaf. It also makes for a large loaf with a small crumb structure, so say goodbye to the tiny slices of holey bread that you might have been tolerating since being gluten-free!

200 g (7 oz) warm water (37–40°C/100–105°F is ideal)
1 tablespoon instant dried yeast
1 tablespoon caster (superfine) sugar
330 g (11⅔ oz) **basic flour blend** (page 18),
  plus extra for dusting
1 tablespoon psyllium husk powder
1 teaspoon xanthan gum
1 teaspoon gluten-free baking powder
¾ teaspoon salt
2 eggs
2 teaspoons runny honey
1 teaspoon apple cider vinegar
60 g (2 oz) unsalted butter, chilled and cubed,
  plus extra for greasing and glazing
1–2 teaspoons vegetable oil
1 egg yolk
2 tablespoons single (light) cream

Add the warm water to a medium jug or bowl, then mix in the yeast and sugar. Cover and leave in a warm, draft-free place for 10 minutes until the yeast has 'bloomed', which means there is a thick layer of foam on the surface. (If a layer of foam has not formed, your yeast may not be active and the bread will not work properly. See page 36 for guidance on working with yeast.)

Meanwhile, combine the flour, psyllium husk, xanthan gum, baking powder and salt in the bowl of a stand mixer.

Whisk the egg into the water-yeast mixture, then pour this into the dry ingredients. Mix slowly (with the paddle attachment) until mostly combined, then mix vigorously (medium speed on a mixer) for 4–5 minutes, scraping down the side of the bowl once or twice to ensure all the ingredients are combining.

When the dough is smooth (it will still be quite wet and sticky), add the cubed butter then continue mixing until no lumps of butter remain.

Grease a large bowl with vegetable oil, then transfer and gather the dough into it. Shake and rotate the bowl a little to ensure the dough is a uniform ball, then flip it over. The aim is to have a smooth ball of dough that is greased all over, not to incorporate more fat into the dough, so try to avoid handling it and dimpling the dough with your fingers. Cover the bowl with cling film (plastic wrap), then a tea towel (dish towel) and place it in a warm, draft-free place for 1 hour.

...continues overleaf

While the dough is proving, grease a 12 × 22 cm (5 × 9 in) loaf tin with butter.

Grease your work surface and hands with a little vegetable oil, then tip out the dough. Knead the dough by hand for 30–40 seconds, removing the air bubbles, until it is a smooth ball of dough.

## TO MAKE A LOAF

Gently roll the ball of dough into a log about 22 cm (9 in) long. Try not to roll or fold the dough in a way that leaves open seams or air pockets as this will affect the shape of the bread as it bakes. Dust the dough and your work surface with a little flour, then roll the log around, just enough to stop it being sticky and to help smooth the surface of the dough. Gently transfer the log of dough into your prepared loaf tin.

## TO MAKE ROLLS

If you're making rolls, roll the dough into a log as above, but before flouring it, simply divide it into 8–12 equal pieces. Roll each piece into a uniform ball, then proceed with a light dusting of flour to help smooth their surfaces. Place the dough balls on a baking sheet lined with baking paper.

Cover the loaf or rolls loosely first with cling film, then a tea towel, and leave in a warm, draft-free place for 15–20 minutes, or until the dough has grown in size by about 75%.

Preheat the oven to 200°C Fan (400°F Fan).

Prepare the egg wash by beating together the egg yolk and cream in a small bowl.

When the dough has proved, gently brush the surface with egg wash, then place in the centre of your oven. Bake the loaf for 20 minutes, then reduce the heat to 160°C Fan (325°F Fan) and bake for a further 70–75 minutes. Bake the rolls for 15–20 minutes, then reduce the heat to 160°C Fan (325°F Fan) and bake for a further 30 minutes.

When cooked, remove the bread from the oven and glaze the top with a knob of butter (this is optional but softens the crust and adds extra flavour and shine). Allow the loaf to cool in the tin for at least 2 hours, and the rolls to cool on the baking sheet for at least 40 minutes. This is essential to set the crumb and prevent the loaf from shrinking and becoming dense or gummy. Transfer the loaf or rolls to a cooling rack and allow to cool for a further 30–60 minutes before slicing.

# CREAMY CHICKEN AND BACON PIES

Serves 6

I don't think a picnic is complete without some form of pastry – be it a pie, sausage roll, or a little something sweet. These make a great addition to a picnic basket (or any kind of meal, for that matter) because they're rich, buttery, very moreish and they travel well.

1 quantity of **puff pastry** (page 106)
unsalted butter, for greasing
1 tablespoon extra virgin olive oil
1 onion, diced
1 small carrot, diced
3–4 garlic cloves, finely chopped
60 g (2 oz) bacon, chopped
1 skinless chicken breast, cut into 2–3 cm (¾–1¼ in) pieces
1 tablespoon gluten-free cornflour (cornstarch)
80 g (2¾ oz) peas (fresh or frozen)
150 ml (5 fl oz) single (light) cream
2 thyme sprigs, leaves picked
1 tablespoon finely chopped parsley
1 egg, beaten
salt and cracked black pepper

Prepare the pastry according to the instructions on page 106. Preheat the oven to 180°C Fan (350°F Fan) and grease 6 holes of a standard-sized muffin tray with butter.

Use a 7–8 cm (2¾–1¼ in) round cookie cutter to cut 6 circles from the dough and set these aside. These will be the tops of the pies. Gather the scraps of the dough and re-roll it to about 3–4 mm (⅛ in) thick. Now use a 9 cm (3½ in) round cookie cutter to cut out another 6 circles. These will make up the base of the pies. Place all the dough circles on a baking sheet and refrigerate until needed.

To make the filling, heat the oil in a large pan set over medium heat, then add the onion and carrot. Cook for 3–4 minutes until softened and translucent, then add the garlic and fry for about 1 minute until fragrant. Place the chicken pieces in a bowl and toss with the cornflour, then add this to the pan and fry until lightly browned on all sides.

Add the peas and cream, then season with plenty of salt and pepper. Bring to a simmer, stirring regularly, until the cream has thickened, then add the herbs. Cook for 2–3 minutes until the chicken is tender and the cream resembles a gravy, thick enough to just bind the ingredients together. Remove from the heat.

Take the pastry from the fridge and gently press the larger circles of dough into the base of the greased muffin tray holes. The pastry should come all the way up the sides of the muffin holes and slightly over the top rim. Prick the base of each one 2–3 times with a fork.

Fill the pastry cases with the chicken mixture. They should be as full to the brim as possible while still able to be covered by the small rounds of pastry.

Top each pie with the remaining circles of pastry, pressing around the edges with a fork to seal the pastry tops to the bases. Brush the tops with a little beaten egg, then use a small, sharp knife to pierce a hole in the top of each pie to release steam during cooking.

Bake for 34–36 minutes, rotating the tray once or twice during cooking if the pastry seems to be browning unevenly. Once cooked, allow to cool in the muffin tray for 15–20 minutes before transferring them to a wire rack to cool. Serve warm or allow to cool completely before storing in an airtight container in the fridge.

# SPICED FRUIT LOAF

Serves 6–8

The incredible smell that wafts from the oven when baking this fruit loaf might be enough reason to make it, even if it wasn't ridiculously tasty. I love to have fresh slices slathered with butter and a little drizzle of honey but it's delicious toasted, too.

220 ml (7½ fl oz) warm water (37–40°C/100–105°F is ideal)
1 tablespoon instant dried yeast
2½ tablespoons caster (superfine) sugar
280 g (10 oz) **basic flour blend** (page 18), plus extra for dusting
1 tablespoon psyllium husk powder
1 teaspoon xanthan gum
1 teaspoon gluten-free baking powder
½ teaspoon salt
1 tablespoon ground cinnamon
1¼ teaspoons ground nutmeg
½ teaspoon ground allspice
½ teaspoon ground ginger
½ teaspoon ground cardamom
100 g (3½ oz) mixed dried fruit
2 eggs
2 teaspoons vanilla bean paste (or extract)
40 g (1½ oz) unsalted butter, chilled and cubed, plus extra for greasing and glazing
1–2 teaspoons vegetable oil
1 egg yolk
2 tablespoons single (light) cream

Add the warm water to a medium jug or bowl, then mix in the yeast and 1½ tablespoons of the sugar. Cover and leave in a warm, draft-free place for 10 minutes until the yeast has 'bloomed', which means there is a thick layer of foam on the surface. (If a layer of foam has not formed, your yeast may not be active and the loaf will not work properly. See page 36 for guidance on working with yeast.)

Meanwhile, combine the flour, psyllium husk powder, xanthan gum, baking powder, salt, spices and the remaining 1 tablespoon of sugar in the bowl of a stand mixer.

In a separate bowl, dust the mixed dried fruit with 2 teaspoons of flour and toss to coat.

Whisk the eggs and vanilla into the water-yeast mixture, then pour this into the dry ingredients. Mix slowly (with the paddle attachment) until mostly combined, then mix vigorously (medium speed on a mixer) for 4–5 minutes, scraping down the side of the bowl once or twice to ensure all the ingredients are combining.

When the dough is smooth (it will still be quite wet and sticky), add the cubed butter and mixed dried fruit, then run the mixer until no lumps of butter remain.

Grease a large bowl with vegetable oil, then transfer and gather the dough into it. Shake and rotate the bowl a little to ensure the dough is a uniform ball, then flip it over. The aim is to have a smooth ball of dough that is greased all over, not to incorporate more fat into the dough, so try to avoid handling it and dimpling the dough with your fingers. Cover the bowl first with cling film (plastic wrap), then with a tea towel (dish towel) and place it in a warm, draft-free place for 1 hour.

While the dough is proofing, grease a 12 × 22 cm (5 × 9 in) loaf tin with butter.

Grease your work surface and hands with a little vegetable oil, then tip out the dough. Knead the dough by hand for 30–40 seconds, removing the air bubbles, until it is a smooth ball of dough.

Gently roll the ball of dough into a log about 22 cm (9 in) long. Try not to roll or fold the dough in a way that leaves open seams or air pockets as this will affect the shape of the bread as it bakes. Dust the dough and your work surface with a little flour, then roll the log around, just enough to stop it being sticky and to help smooth the surface of the dough. Gently transfer the log of dough into your prepared loaf tin.

Cover the loaf loosely first with cling film, then a tea towel, and leave in a warm, draft-free place for 45–60 minutes, or the dough has grown in size by about 75%.

Preheat the oven to 160°C Fan (325°F Fan).

Prepare the egg wash by beating together the egg yolk and cream in a small bowl.

When the loaf has proved, gently brush the surface with the egg wash, then bake in the centre of the oven for 60–70 minutes until it is a rich brown colour (but not burned).

When cooked, remove the loaf from the oven and glaze the top with a knob of butter (this is optional but softens the crust and adds extra flavour and shine). Allow the loaf to cool in the tin for at least 2 hours. This is essential to set the crumb and prevent the loaf from shrinking and becoming dense or gummy. Remove from the tin and transfer to a cooling rack for a further 1 hour before slicing.

NOTE

*This loaf also makes great crackers for a cheeseboard. Simply slice it very thinly and bake the slices in the oven low and slow at 120°C Fan (250°F Fan) for 60–70 minutes until crisp.*

# CINNAMON ROLLS

Makes 9

These are the cinnamon rolls I hunted for *desperately* in the years after my coeliac diagnosis. Funnily enough, cinnamon rolls weren't even one of my favourite things when I could eat gluten, but when it was taken off the table, cravings for those soft, sweet rolls really kicked in and I couldn't find a good substitute anywhere. Until I made these! This dough is versatile and works for lots of different recipes, both sweet and savoury, but these cinnamon rolls should definitely be the first thing you make. They're perfectly sweet and squishy and will be an excellent addition to your picnic spread.

200 g (7 oz) warm water (37–40°C/100–105°F is ideal)
1 tablespoon instant dried yeast
60 g (2 oz) caster (superfine) sugar
280 g (10 oz) **basic flour blend** (page 18), plus extra for dusting
3½ teaspoons psyllium husk powder
1 teaspoon xanthan gum
1 teaspoon gluten-free baking powder
½ teaspoon salt
2 eggs
40 g (1½ oz) butter, chilled and cubed
vegetable oil, for greasing

**For the filling**
140 g (5 oz) soft light brown sugar
1½ tablespoons ground cinnamon
¼ teaspoon salt
85 g (3 oz) unsalted butter, softened

**For the cream cheese frosting**
25 g (1 oz) unsalted butter
120 g (4 oz) cream cheese
100 g (3½ oz) icing (powdered) sugar, sifted
pinch of salt
¼ teaspoon vanilla bean paste (or extract)

Add the warm water to a medium jug or bowl, then mix in the yeast and 30 g (1 oz) of the sugar. Cover and leave in a warm, draft-free place for 10 minutes until the yeast has 'bloomed', which means there is a thick layer of foam on the surface. (If a layer of foam has not formed, your yeast may not be active and the rolls will not work properly. See page 36 for guidance on working with yeast.)

Meanwhile, combine the flour, psyllium husk powder, xanthan gum, baking powder, salt and the remaining 30 g (1 oz) sugar in the bowl of a stand mixer.

Whisk the egg into the water-yeast mixture, then pour this into the dry ingredients. Mix slowly (with the paddle attachment) until mostly combined, then mix vigorously (medium speed on a mixer) for 3–4 minutes, scraping down the side of the bowl once or twice to ensure all the ingredients are combining.

Add the cubed butter and continue mixing on medium speed for 5–6 minutes, stopping two or three times to scrape down the side of the bowl. When the dough is ready it will be very sticky but smooth, and you should be able to use a dough scraper or spatula to scrape it into a single ball.

Grease a large bowl with vegetable oil, then transfer and gather the dough into it. Shake and rotate the bowl a little to ensure the dough is a uniform ball, then flip it over. The aim is to have a smooth ball of dough that is greased all over, not to incorporate more fat into the dough, so try to avoid handling it and dimpling the dough with your fingers. Cover the bowl with cling film (plastic wrap) and place it in a warm, draft-free place for 1 hour until doubled in size.

...continues overleaf

Meanwhile, prepare the filling. In a small bowl, mix the brown sugar, cinnamon and salt in a small bowl and set aside.

Line a 22 cm (9 in) square baking tin with baking paper.

Grease your work surface and hands with a little vegetable oil, then tip out the dough. Knead the dough by hand for 30–40 seconds, removing the air bubbles, until it is a smooth ball of dough.

Dust the work surface and the dough quite generously with flour, then roll it into a 40 × 30 cm (16 × 12 in) rectangle, with a long side facing you.

Spread the softened butter over the dough, doing your best not to pull it too much or rip holes in it (this is not difficult if the butter is softened). Leave a 2–3 cm (¾–1½ in) strip unbuttered along the top edge of the dough but spread the butter right to the edges of the other 3 sides. Sprinkle the cinnamon sugar over the butter in an even layer, then pat it gently into the butter.

Starting with the edge closest to you, roll the dough up into a log. Do this as tightly as you can while avoiding stretching the dough (it is more delicate than a gluten-filled dough).

Using a sharp serrated knife, cut the log into 9 equal portions, each about 4–5 cm (1½–2 in) wide (cutting them using floss or twine will create neater rolls, but it is not essential). Arrange them in the prepared baking tin, slightly space apart. Cover the dish first with cling film, then with a tea towel (dish towel), and leave to prove in a warm, draft-free place for 15–20 minutes, or until the buns have grown in size by about 75%.

Preheat the oven to 160°C Fan (325°F Fan).

Bake the rolls for 35–40 minutes, until they're golden brown all over.

Meanwhile, make the cream cheese frosting by whisking all the ingredients together in a medium bowl. Refrigerate until ready to use.

Remove the rolls from the oven and allow them to cool in the tin for 25–30 minutes, then take them out of the tray (do this while the rolls are warm as the sugar will harden in the base of the tin as it cools, sticking the rolls in place).

When the rolls have cooled completely, top them with the cream cheese frosting and serve. These will keep in an airtight container in the fridge for 1–2 days or in the freezer (unfrosted) for up to 2 months (simply reheat them in the microwave then frost once cool).

# CHOCOLATE CUPCAKES WITH PEANUT BUTTER CARAMEL

Makes 12

These might be some of the richest, most decadent chocolate cupcakes I've ever had! Chocolate is delicious, of course, but pairing it with my peanut butter caramel takes these cupcakes to a whole other level.

190 g (6¾ oz) caster (superfine) sugar
2 eggs
2 teaspoons vanilla bean paste (or extract)
80 ml (2¾ fl oz) vegetable oil
1 teaspoon apple cider vinegar
50 g (1¾ oz) **basic flour blend** (page 18), plus extra for dusting
60 g (2 oz) rice flour
50 g (1¾ oz) unsweetened cocoa powder
1½ teaspoons gluten-free baking powder
⅓ teaspoon salt
150 ml (5 fl oz) boiling water

**For the peanut butter caramel**
120 g (4¼ oz) caster (superfine) sugar
2 tablespoons cold water
90 ml (3 fl oz) single (light) cream
15 g (½ oz) unsalted butter
⅛ teaspoon salt
60 g (2 oz) smooth peanut butter

**For the chocolate buttercream**
200 g (7 oz) unsalted butter
200 g (7 oz) icing (powdered) sugar
15 g (½ oz) unsweetened cocoa powder
1 teaspoon vanilla bean paste (or extract)
½ teaspoon salt

Preheat the oven to 160°C Fan (325°F Fan) and line a 12-hole muffin tray with cupcake cases.

Add the sugar, eggs, vanilla, oil and vinegar to a large mixing bowl and beat with a hand-held electric beater (or use a stand mixer) until pale and fluffy.

Sift the dry ingredients into the bowl and mix until just combined. Then add the boiling water and fold it into the batter with a spatula. Divide the batter between the muffin holes and bake in the centre of the oven for 18–20 minutes until a skewer inserted into a cupcake comes out clean (some cooked crumbs or moisture is fine, just no cake batter).

Allow the cupcakes to cool in the muffin tray for 15–20 minutes before transferring them to a cooling rack to cool completely.

While the cupcakes are cooling, make the peanut butter caramel. Add the sugar and cold water to a medium saucepan, agitating it slightly until all the sugar has been moistened. Place over medium heat, bring it to the boil and allow it to simmer (without touching it!) for 6–7 minutes, checking continuously to ensure it is not changing colour.

Pour the cream into a microwave-safe jug (pitcher) and microwave on high (900W) for 30–45 seconds. As the colour of the sugar starts to change, reduce the heat to low and watch it constantly. As soon as it becomes a rich, amber colour remove it from the heat and pour in the hot cream. Be careful as it will bubble vigorously and release a lot of very hot steam. As soon as possible, whisk to combine the

...continues overleaf

caramel with the cream. If it is not coming together, place back over low heat and whisk until combined. Remove from the heat and whisk in the butter and salt. Once combined, whisk in the peanut butter until smooth. Pour into a clean bowl to cool and set aside.

When the cupcakes and caramel have cooled, make the buttercream frosting. In a large bowl, beat the butter with a hand-held electric beater (or use a stand mixer) on a medium-high speed for 5–6 minutes until pale and fluffy. Add the remaining ingredients and continue mixing on a high speed for a further 5–6 minutes. The buttercream should be light and airy. Transfer to a piping bag fitted with a star nozzle and set aside.

Using a teaspoon or apple corer, scoop out a portion of sponge from the top of each cupcake so that there's a small hollow, ideally 2–3 cm (¾–1½ in) deep. Fill each hollow to the brim with the caramel. Pipe the buttercream onto each cupcake (you can also spoon it on if you prefer) to finish. Eat immediately or store in a sealed container in the fridge until ready to transport, or for up to 4–5 days (the buttercream will soften or melt if left in very warm conditions; if chilled, allow it to come to room temperature before using).

NOTE

*To make these nut-allergy friendly, simply omit the peanut butter in the caramel and replace it with an extra 1 tablespoon of butter. You can also leave out the caramel altogether – the chocolatey flavour alone will satisfy even the hungriest of cupcake fans.*

# GAME DAY FEAST

Regardless of the game that's playing, big sporting events are always a great reason to gather your friends and family. I love playing host on these days because the alternative often means missing out on food, which is a really big part of the occasion. For this feast, I've put together a spread that'll have people dashing from the tv to the table, not wanting to miss the action at either. You'll find all the classics you'd expect to see on the table for the big game, but with none of the gluten and plenty more flavour.

# GARLIC BREAD (BUT BETTER)

Serves 4–5

I know it's a bold claim to say that any kind of garlic bread is better than the classic we all know and love but, *I promise*, this recipe delivers. It's got all the best aspects of the regular version – fragrant garlic, plenty of butter and some herbs for freshness – but it's also deliciously creamy and cheesy, and the caramelised leeks provide some sweetness and texture. In fact, I'd highly recommend you overestimate how much you think you're going to need to feed everyone because I guarantee people will be reaching for seconds … and thirds.

1 tablespoon extra virgin olive oil
1 leek, finely sliced
¼ teaspoon salt
4–6 garlic cloves, minced
80 g (2¾ oz) salted butter, softened, plus extra for frying
50 g (1¾ oz) cream cheese
1 tablespoon finely chopped parsley
about 8 slices of gluten-free white bread (see page 118 for homemade)
2–3 tablespoons freshly grated Parmesan

Preheat the oven to 220°C Fan (425°F Fan) and line a large baking sheet with baking paper.

Add the oil, 1 tablespoon of extra butter, the leek and salt to a large frying pan (skillet) and set it over medium-low heat. Cook gently for 4–5 minutes, stirring regularly. When the leek has softened, add the garlic and continue to cook, stirring regularly, for 10–12 minutes until the leek has caramelised and the mixture is fragrant.

While the leek is cooking, combine the butter, cream cheese and parsley in a bowl.

When the leek is cooked, combine it with the cream cheese mixture and stir well.

Arrange the bread slices in a single layer on the baking sheet and bake for 2–3 minutes on each side until slightly crisp. Remove from the oven and spread an even layer of the leek mixture onto each slice. Sprinkle each slice with Parmesan, then return the garlic bread to the oven for 8–10 minutes, or until lightly browned.

Allow to cool on the tray for a few minutes before transferring to a plate to serve.

# SWEET SPICED PORK RIBS

Serves 4–6

The spices and sticky sweet glaze on these pork ribs make them the perfect finger food for game day. They're cooked low and slow to keep them tender, juicy and easy to eat off the bone. It's also really easy to scale this recipe, so whether you're feeding a crowd or just a few friends, they are always going to hit the spot.

2 kg (4¼ lb) pork rib racks
1 teaspoon salt
½ teaspoon white pepper
1 teaspoon garlic powder
½ teaspoon Chinese five spice
3 tablespoons soft light brown sugar
120 ml (4 fl oz) runny honey
120 ml (4 fl oz) tomato ketchup
2 tablespoons gochujang paste or sriracha (optional)
1 tablespoon sesame oil
2 teaspoons gluten-free soy sauce

Preheat the oven to 140°C Fan (275°F Fan).

Prepare a sheet of foil for each rack of ribs, each sheet large enough to encase a rack. Now place a smaller sheet of baking paper in the centre of each sheet of foil. Place a rack of ribs on each.

In a small bowl, combine the salt, white pepper, garlic powder, Chinese five spice and 1 tablespoon of brown sugar. Sprinkle this sparingly onto each side of the pork rib racks, massaging it into the meat as you go.

In another bowl, combine the rest of the ingredients, including the remaining 2 tablespoons of brown sugar, to make the sauce. Mix well, then transfer about one-third of this sauce to a separate bowl (you'll use this later). Use a silicone brush to coat the rib racks on all sides with the remaining sauce.

Seal each of the ribs racks in the foil, adding foil to the top side of the ribs if necessary to encase each one in its own foil and baking paper parcel. Place the parcels on baking trays and bake for 90 minutes.

After 90 minutes, remove the trays from the oven, then increase the oven temperature to 220°C Fan (425°F Fan). Open the foil packages to expose the ribs, then brush the reserved sauce all over them. Return the exposed ribs to the oven (don't seal the foil) and bake for a further 10–15 minutes until the sauce caramelises and becomes sticky.

Allow the ribs to cool slightly, then use a sharp knife to slice between the individual ribs. Transfer to a platter and serve while hot.

# PRAWN ROLLS WITH ROASTED GARLIC MAYO

Makes 12

These are inspired by lobster rolls with the aim of making them a little more budget friendly, especially if feeding a crowd. Poaching the prawns keeps them plump, sweet and juicy, so no-one is going to mind the switch, I promise. Especially not when stuffed generously into a fresh, soft roll with a delicious homemade garlic mayonnaise.

1 whole garlic bulb
1 teaspoon extra virgin olive oil
12 **sandwich loaf rolls** (page 118), or use store-bought gluten-free mini hot dog buns
1–2 heads butterhead lettuce
salt and cracked black pepper

**For the mayonnaise**
1 egg
½ teaspoon salt
1½ tablespoons lemon juice
1 teaspoon Dijon mustard
200 ml (7 fl oz) vegetable oil

**For the prawns**
1 unwaxed lemon, sliced
500 g (18 oz) prawns (shrimp), peeled and deveined
small handful of chives, finely chopped

Preheat the oven to 200°C Fan (400°F Fan).

Slice the top off the garlic bulb and place it on a sheet of foil. Drizzle the garlic bulb with 1 teaspoon of olive oil and season it with salt and pepper, then wrap it up in the foil. Roast for 30–45 minutes. (You can roast it in the oven while the rolls bake.)

Next, make the mayonnaise. In the canister of a stick blender or a tall jug (pitcher), place the egg, salt, lemon juice, mustard and vegetable oil. Unwrap the garlic from the foil and squeeze the flesh into the canister or jug, too. Place the stick blender all the way into the canister (or jug) so it sits on the bottom, then blitz, without moving it, until the egg emulsifies with the oil. Now very slowly move the stick blender (while still blitzing) upwards through the rest of the ingredients until you have a homogenous, thick mayonnaise. (Alternatively, you can use a blender or food processor – to do so, start by mixing the above ingredients without the vegetable oil, then slowly trickle the oil in as you mix.) Set aside.

Next prep the prawns. Place a large saucepan of water over high heat. Season generously with salt (as you would for pasta), then add 4–5 slices of fresh lemon. Fill a large bowl two-thirds full with water and ice cubes.

When the water on the stove is at a rapid boil, turn off the heat and immediately add the prawns. Place the lid on the saucepan and poach the prawns for 2–3 minutes, until they're just cooked through. They should be plump and juicy. Use a slotted spoon to transfer the prawns directly to the ice bath.

When the prawns are cool, chop them into smaller pieces and add them to a bowl along

pictured overleaf

with enough of the garlic mayo to generously coat the prawns. Add most of the chopped chives and mix well.

Cut the rolls open at the top like hot dog buns and place 1–2 leaves of lettuce in each. Spoon in some of the prawn mixture, then top with the remaining chopped chives before serving.

NOTE

*For this recipe you will need to make 12 bread rolls according to the recipe on page 118. However, instead of rolling the dough into balls, roll each portion of dough into mini log shapes instead, with slightly tapered ends.*

# GINGER AND SESAME SLAW

Serves 4–6

**This is a super-simple, crowd-pleasing salad packed full of flavour and crunch! Make the slaw ahead of time, as well as the dressing, but keep them separate until ready to serve. This way, you can make it a day in advance and have everything fresh when it's time to feed your friends and family.**

1 small red cabbage (or half a large one), finely shredded
2 carrots, peeled and finely shredded
200 g (7 oz) fresh beansprouts
small handful coriander (cilantro) leaves, roughly chopped (optional)
1 teaspoon grated fresh ginger
1 tablespoon runny honey
3 tablespoons gluten-free soy sauce
1 tablespoon sesame oil

In a large mixing bowl, toss together the vegetables and coriander until well combined.

In a small jar or bowl, combine the ginger, honey, soy sauce and sesame oil. Shake the jar or whisk vigorously until the oil emulsifies to create a dressing.

When ready to serve, pour the dressing over the vegetables and toss to combine.

pictured on page 144

# CHEESEBURGER SLIDERS WITH KIMCHI SLAW

Makes 12

I love making sliders for large groups because they're a relatively fuss-free option that everyone enjoys. This recipe is mainly about the deliciously soft and bready homemade buns paired with the tangy kimchi slaw, so I've left the rest up to you to customise with your favourite burger fillings. My top hack for sliders is to buy some delicious meatballs and then squash them into a frying pan, like smash burgers. This makes the perfect size patties and means you can use whatever variety you like – whether it's beef, chicken, or a vegan option.

vegetable oil, for frying
10 meatballs of your choice
12 **sandwich loaf rolls** (page 118), or use store-bought gluten-free mini burger buns
cheese of your choice, sliced
burger pickles
1 cucumber, sliced

**For the kimchi slaw**
1 garlic clove, minced
3 tablespoons gluten-free Kewpie mayonnaise
½ teaspoon sesame oil
1 teaspoon white rice vinegar
⅛ teaspoon salt
½ teaspoon runny honey
1 teaspoon gluten-free gochujang paste
1–2 teaspoon chilli oil (optional but recommended)
¼ green cabbage, shredded
1 spring onion (scallion), finely sliced
½ carrot, peeled and shredded
150 g (5½ oz) gluten-free kimchi, roughly chopped

To make the slaw, add the garlic, Kewpie, sesame oil, vinegar, salt, honey, gochujang and chilli oil (if using) to a large bowl and whisk well to combine. Now add the cabbage, spring onion, carrot and kimchi and toss until everything is well combined. Set aside while you cook the burgers.

Add a little vegetable oil to a large frying pan (skillet) and set it over medium-high heat. Place the meatballs into the pan and press them down firmly with a spatula to squash them into patties (you may have to do this in batches). Cook the patties for 2 minutes, then flip them and top each one with a slice of cheese. Cook for 2 more minutes until the cheese is melted and the patty is cooked through, then remove them from the pan.

Halve the bread rolls and toast them gently in the pan you just used to fry the patties.

To assemble, place a patty on the base of a roll. Top with pickles, freshly sliced cucumber and a spoonful of slaw. Add the top of the bun and transfer to a large board for serving.

NOTE

*For this recipe you will need to make 12 bread rolls according to the recipe on page 118.*

# CRUNCHY FRIED CHICKEN WINGS

Serves 3–4

I've served these to countless groups of friends and they're one of my most-requested dishes. The coating is crisp and delicious, and soaks up so much flavour from the sweet, spicy sauce. The marinade also helps to keep the wings juicy on the inside, so these really do hit all the right spots.

neutral oil, for shallow frying
2 spring onions (scallions), sliced
toasted sesame seeds
salt

**For the chicken**
1 kg (35 oz) chicken wings
3 garlic cloves, minced
2 teaspoons grated fresh ginger
2 teaspoons caster (superfine) sugar
2 tablespoons sake (or other rice wine)
2 tablespoons gluten-free soy sauce
1 tablespoon lemon juice

**For the coating**
150 g (5½ oz) rice flour
150 g (5½ oz) potato starch
½ teaspoon white pepper

**For the sauce**
2 tablespoons sesame oil
3 garlic cloves, minced
1 teaspoon grated fresh ginger
4 tablespoons runny honey
1 tablespoon gluten-free gochujang paste or sriracha (or other hot sauce)
80 ml (2¾ fl oz) cold water

Start by marinating the chicken. Place the wings in a large bowl and add all the other ingredients. Mix well with your hands, then cover and refrigerate for at least 30 minutes (several hours is preferable).

In a medium bowl, combine the coating ingredients, along with ½ teaspoon of salt, and mix well. Working with several pieces of chicken at a time, toss them in the flour mix to ensure they're well coated on all sides. Transfer the floured chicken to a clean plate.

Place 2 cm (¾ in) of neutral oil in a large, deep frying pan (skillet) and set over medium-high heat. Check the oil temperature – when you're ready to fry it should be hot enough that a wooden chopstick or wooden spoon sizzles when dipped into the oil.

Working in batches, shake any excess flour off the wings, then place them into the hot oil. Fry them for 8–10 minutes, turning them regularly to ensure they brown evenly.

While the wings are frying, make the sauce. In a small saucepan, combine the sesame oil, garlic and ginger. Place the pan over medium heat and cook for 1–2 minutes until fragrant. Add the honey and gochujang and stir to combine, then mix in the water. Reduce the heat to low and simmer for 2–3 minutes, then season with salt to taste and remove it from the heat.

As the chicken pieces finish cooking, transfer them to a wire rack to drain excess oil. Once all the chicken is cooked, place the wings in a large bowl and drizzle over the sauce (it thickens as it cools so it may need to be reheated slightly before pouring over the chicken – it should be sticky but runny). Toss well to coat the wings in the sauce.

Transfer the coated wings to a serving dish, then top with spring onions and scatter over toasted sesame seeds before serving.

NOTE

*I shallow fry these, so smaller wing pieces are ideal. I like to buy wings that have already had the wingettes (the flatter, double-boned section) separated from the drumettes (the meatier piece that attaches the wing to the chicken frame), or I butcher them myself. You can use whole wings but bear in mind that you'll need to fry them in more oil, and they will take longer to cook. You can also use an air fryer for the wings if you prefer – just follow the air fryer guidelines for cooking chicken.*

# MINI APPLE PIES

### Makes 10

Upon perfecting my puff pastry, of course I *had* to make apple pies. And I do prefer mini handheld pies because I think the pastry to filling ratio is much more satisfying! These are super buttery and very moreish. They also happen to be ideal for a gameday feast because you can prep them ahead of time and keep them in the fridge until you're ready to bake and serve.

1 quantity of **puff pastry dough** (page 106)
1 egg, beaten

**For the filling**
2 Granny Smith apples, peeled, cored and chopped
25 g (1 oz) unsalted butter
2 teaspoons soft light brown sugar
¼ teaspoon ground cinnamon
2 tablespoons cold water
⅛ teaspoon salt (or to taste)
1 teaspoon gluten-free cornflour (cornstarch)

**For the icing**
80 g (2¾ oz) icing (powdered) sugar
¼ teaspoon ground cinnamon
1 tablespoon boiling water

Prepare the puff pastry according to the directions on page 106. When rolling it out for the final time, instead of stopping when the pastry measures 22 × 36 cm (8¾ × 14 in), roll it a little thinner, to a rectangle that measures 24 × 40 cm (9½ × 16 in).

Along a short edge, make 3 cuts spaced 6 cm (2¼ in) apart. Along a long edge, make 4 cuts spaced 8 cm (3¼ in) apart. Cut along these marks to give you 20 small rectangles of pastry. Cover and refrigerate until needed.

Preheat the oven to 180°C Fan (350°F Fan) and line a baking sheet with baking paper.

Place all the filling ingredients in a medium saucepan set over medium heat. Mix well and allow to cook for 5–10 minutes until the apples are tender and the liquid has thickened. Remove from the heat.

Take the pastry from the fridge and spoon some of the apple filling onto 10 of the rectangles. Use a pastry brush to brush a little beaten egg onto the pastry around the apple filling, then take an empty piece of pastry and place it over the filling, lining the edges up with the pastry at the base. Gently press the pastry down around the filling, then press the edges down with a fork to join the pastry pieces.

Place the pies onto the prepared baking sheet and brush each with a little egg. Use a sharp knife to pierce the top of each pie to release steam during cooking.

Bake for 34–36 minutes until the pies have browned and puffed nicely. Remove from the oven and transfer to a wire rack to cool for at least 10–15 minutes.

To make the icing, in a small bowl combine the icing sugar and cinnamon. Add the boiling water and stir until smooth, then drizzle the icing over the finished apple pies.

NOTE

*You can prep these in advance and freeze them before baking. For best results, allow them to thaw in the fridge and then bake as directed.*

# S'MORES CHOCOLATE SLICE

Serves 8–10

This is a great sweet option for a game day feast because it's a tasty, simple dessert that can be made ahead of time. It's also easy to eat by hand, meaning you can serve it on a platter and allow your guests to help themselves. While the inspiration for this slice is the classic s'more, made with marshmallows, I elevate mine a little by topping the slice with Swiss meringue instead. This is a silky toasted meringue that is reminiscent of melted marshmallows without the overwhelming sticky sweetness that can sometimes overpower the chocolate-biscuit combo.

**For the biscuit base**
1 quantity of **sweet pastry dough** (page 103)
or
300 g (10½ oz) rich tea biscuits, digestive biscuits or graham crackers

**For the chocolate**
90 g (3 oz) salted butter, melted
150 g (5½ oz) milk chocolate, chopped
50 g (1¾ oz) dark (bittersweet) chocolate, chopped
100 ml (3⅓ fl oz) single (light) cream

**For the 'marshmallow'**
2 egg whites
70 g (2½ oz) caster (superfine) sugar
⅛ teaspoon cream of tartar
1 teaspoon vanilla bean paste (or extract)

Preheat the oven to 160°C Fan (325°F) Fan and line a large baking sheet with baking paper.

If using, make the sweet pastry dough according to the instructions on page 106, stopping before the refrigeration step. Instead of wrapping in cling film (plastic wrap), crumble the pastry directly onto the lined baking sheet. Bake for 25–30 minutes, or until the pastry is golden brown (some lighter patches are fine, as long as the dough is cooked). Allow to cool for 20–30 minutes.

Line a rectangular baking dish (about 16 × 24 cm/ 6 × 9½ in) with baking paper, ensuring there is plenty of overhang so you can lift it later.

Add the baked pastry pieces or the biscuits/ crackers to a food processor. Blitz to a fine crumb and transfer to a mixing bowl along with the melted butter and mix well to moisten all the crumbs. Tip the mixture into the lined baking dish, then spread it out into an even layer, using a palette knife or spatula to compress it into a firm base. Place this in the fridge to firm up for 15–20 minutes.

Place both chocolates and the cream into a microwave-safe bowl. Heat in the microwave on high (900W) for 30 seconds, then stir with a spatula. Repeat once or twice more if necessary to melt the chocolate enough so that you can stir the mixture into a smooth ganache. Pour the ganache over the biscuit base, spreading it into an even layer, then place back in the fridge to firm up for 3–4 hours.

To make the Swiss meringue 'marshmallow', first prepare a double boiler or bain-marie set over medium heat. Place the egg whites, sugar and cream of tartar in a large heatproof bowl or the bowl of your stand mixer. Whisk by hand briefly to combine, then place the bowl on the double boiler and whisk constantly until the sugar has dissolved and the temperature of the egg whites reaches 60°C (140°F) on a sugar thermometer.

Remove the bowl from the heat and whisk with a hand-held electric beater or stand mixer on a low–medium speed for 1–2 minutes. Now, increase the speed to high and whisk until medium peaks form (the meringue should be very thick and glossy). Add the vanilla and continue whisking on high speed until stiff peaks form (this can take 10–15 minutes, depending on your mixer).

Spoon the meringue onto the ganache layer, spreading it out evenly and swirling it as you spread to make it look pretty. Use a kitchen blowtorch to gently brown the meringue all over the top (or see Note).

Allow the meringue to cool, then carefully lift the giant s'more from the dish using the baking paper and transfer it to a chopping board. Use a hot, sharp knife to cut it into 8–10 pieces, wiping the knife between each cut for neat edges. Serve immediately or store in the fridge (it is best if removed from the fridge at least half an hour before serving).

NOTE

*This recipe asks you to use a kitchen blowtorch. If you don't have one, you can use the grill (broiler) setting on your oven instead. In this case, before adding your meringue layer on top of the ganache, place the baking dish with the crumb and ganache layers in the freezer for 10–15 minutes while you preheat the grill. Now quickly add the meringue, ensuring the ganache is completely covered (this will stop the ganache from melting). Place it under the grill and watch it very closely. It will only need a couple of minutes and can burn very quickly. Turn the dish as necessary so that the meringue browns evenly.*

# TACO NIGHT FEAST

The thing I love most about a taco night is the communal messiness – the fun in sitting around a heavily-laden dinner table with family or friends, all getting involved with dinner. Although tacos can be quite accessible for gluten-free people, there are elements I've included in this feast that we do usually miss out on, like beautifully soft and pliable flour tortillas, or a crunchy golden batter for an epic fish taco. This means that everyone can enjoy a feast together, no-one misses out and absolutely no-one misses the gluten! The following recipes are a collection of my favourite taco fillings and toppings and, no matter how you pile them into a tortilla, they're delicious – feel free to make them your own and find your favourite combos. All the recipes have come directly from the many taco nights I've thrown with friends, which might be why I feel that sharing these recipes is like inviting you around for dinner – I hope you'll enjoy the flavours, abundance, and messiness as much as I do!

# FLOUR TORTILLAS

Makes 12

I've been obsessed with these tortillas since I perfected them! I'd say they get made in my house at least once a week because they're incredibly simple, delicious and so perfectly pliable. Obviously, they're excellent for tacos but if you make them larger, they also work beautifully for burritos and wraps. They're flexible, even quite stretchy, and most importantly, they don't break apart and crumble the second you try to use them. I like to include both these and traditional corn tortillas in my taco night feast but, as corn tortillas are naturally gluten free anyway, they are pretty easy to buy (and there are plenty of recipes for them online already if you want to make them!). Variety or not, you definitely won't feel like you're missing out in anyway if there's a stack of these tortillas in the middle of your taco night feast.

1½ teaspoons lard
120 ml (4 fl oz) warm water
⅓ teaspoon salt
½ teaspoon runny honey
1½ teaspoons psyllium husk powder
90 g (3 oz) **basic flour blend** (page 18), plus extra for dusting

Place the lard in a medium bowl and microwave it for 30–40 seconds until melted. Add the warm water, salt and honey and stir to dissolve, then whisk in the psyllium husk powder. Set the bowl aside for 2–3 minutes until the mixture has thickened into a gel.

Add the flour and mix well with a spatula until fully incorporated (you can use the paddle attachment on a stand mixer, but it only takes a minute or two of mixing by hand).

Generously flour your work surface, then turn the dough out and flour the dough, too. The dough will be very sticky as it is a high hydration dough (meaning the ratio of water to flour is quite high). Roll the dough into a log shape, then divide it into 12 equal portions (each one should weigh 18–20 g/⅔ oz).

Working with one portion at a time, roll the dough into a ball, then use a rolling pin to roll it out into a rough circle, about 16 cm (6 in) in diameter. As you roll, dust more flour on both sides of the tortilla to keep it from sticking to your work surface. It also helps to flip and turn the dough once or twice as you roll it out. It will be quite thin but strong enough for you to gently pick it up and move it around. Now use a large cookie cutter a little smaller than the size of the tortilla (or trace around a bowl with a sharp knife) to cut the tortilla into a perfect circle – this is optional but makes for a neat tortilla. You can collect and re-roll the scraps if you do this.

...continues overleaf

To cook the tortillas, heat a large non-stick frying pan (skillet) over medium heat. When the pan is hot, add as many tortillas as will fit in your pan without overlapping. Cook them for 2–3 minutes, flipping them 3–4 times. Gently press down on the tortillas with a spatula a few times as they cook to help them cook evenly and encourage them to puff up. You should get some patches of golden brown on each side. If any flour in your pan starts to burn or smoke, wipe it out with paper towel between batches.

As soon as each tortilla is cooked, immediately stack and wrap them in a clean tea towel (dish towel). Do not skip this step as the steam and moisture that accumulates helps to make the tortillas perfectly soft and pliable. Serve and enjoy while warm!

NOTE

*If the cooked tortillas are a little crisp, it means that not enough heat and steam was trapped in the tea towel as they cooled. To fix this, ensure the stack is well-wrapped in the tea towel, then pat 1–2 tablespoons of water around the outside of the bundle. Microwave (in the tea towel) on high (900 W) for 30–40 seconds. This will introduce the steam needed to soften them. Don't unwrap the tortillas until it's time to serve. You can also use this method to reheat the tortillas!*

# QUICK PICKLED RED ONIONS

Serves 4–6

**In my opinion, no taco is complete without some pickled red onions. They provide the perfect level of acidity to balance out the richness of the other fillings. I highly recommend making these in a larger quantity and keeping them handy in your fridge as they're a delicious addition to many dishes, even just simple salads or sandwiches.**

1 large red onion, sliced
130 ml (4¼ fl oz) white vinegar
100 ml (3⅓ fl oz) water
2 tablespoons caster (superfine) sugar
⅓ teaspoon salt

Place the sliced onion in a heatproof bowl.

In a small saucepan, combine the vinegar, water, sugar and salt. Place over medium-high heat until the sugar and salt have dissolved.

Pour the hot pickling liquid over the onion. Make sure all the onion is submerged, then allow to cool. Allow the onion to pickle for at least 30 minutes before serving.

You can transfer the onion and its pickling liquid to a sterilised jar to store in the fridge for several weeks.

# AVOCADO AND LIME CREMA

Serves 4–6

I love to include a creamy element with my taco feast. This adds flavour of course, but it's also about making sure all the textural components are there. And as this spread doesn't typically include any melted cheese, the natural fattiness of the avocado (along with the tangy sour cream) is especially welcome here!

Add all the ingredients to a blender or food processor and blitz until smooth, scraping the side as necessary. Season to taste with salt, then transfer to a bowl to serve.

1 ripe avocado, peeled and destoned
1 garlic clove
3 tablespoons sour cream (or Greek yogurt)
2 tablespoons lime juice
¼ teaspoon salt, plus extra to taste

# PICO DE GALLO (CHUNKY TOMATO SALSA)

Serves 4–6

1 sweet white onion or small red onion, finely chopped
1 jalapeño, deseeded and finely chopped (optional)
2 tablespoons fresh lime juice
¾ teaspoon salt, plus extra to taste
6 small tomatoes (or 3–4 medium sized), base and stem removed then diced
generous handful of coriander (cilantro), finely chopped

In a medium bowl, combine the onion and jalapeño (if using) with the lime juice and salt. Allow it to sit for a couple of minutes.

Now add the tomatoes and coriander to the bowl and mix well. Season to taste with salt, then set aside until serving. The flavour will improve with time, so feel free to make this a little ahead of dinner.

# GRILLED PINEAPPLE SALSA

Serves 4–6

**This salsa adds a really nice sweet and smoky flavour to any taco. The acidity of the pineapple helps to cut through the richness of meat, especially pork.**

1 fresh, ripe pineapple
1 chipotle pepper in adobo (with sauce – see Note on page 168)
¼ teaspoon salt, plus extra to taste
¼ teaspoon caster (superfine) sugar (optional)

Start by removing the leaves and cutting off the top and bottom of the pineapple. Remove the skin with a knife, then quarter the pineapple lengthways. Cut off the segment of core on the inside of each quarter.

Heat a frying pan (skillet) over medium-high heat and add the pineapple pieces. Allow them to char before rotating to get a good amount of colour on all sides. This may take 5–10 minutes.

Place the pineapple pieces in a blender or food processor with the chilli (along with some of the adobo sauce) and salt. Pulse into a slightly chunky sauce, then season with salt and a little sugar to taste if necessary. Transfer to a jug or bowl for serving.

NOTE

*I include a little sugar in the salsa to bring out the sweetness of the pineapple. Of course, the flavour of any fruit varies throughout the year so omit or add to taste!*

# SPICED BATTERED COD (OR MUSHROOMS)

Serves 4–6

This battered fish is perfectly light and crisp and probably my favourite taco filling of all. Paired with salsa (opposite), pickled onions (page 161) and fresh coriander, it hits all the spots in terms of flavour and textures. It's also a delicious option to use as a vegan alternative if you use oyster mushrooms instead of fish.

350 g (12¼ oz) boneless cod fillets
or
150–200 g (5½–7 oz) oyster mushrooms

30 g (1 oz) **basic flour blend** (page 18)
60 g (2 oz) gluten-free cornflour (cornstarch)
½ teaspoon salt
¼ teaspoon gluten-free baking powder
¼ teaspoon smoked paprika
¼ teaspoon ground cumin
¼ teaspoon garlic powder
150 ml (4¼ fl oz) chilled water
neutral oil, for frying

Slice the cod fillets into 7–8 cm (2¾–3¼ in) long batons (or separate the oyster mushrooms into large, bite size pieces). Place between sheets of paper towel to draw out as much excess moisture as possible.

Place all the dry ingredients into a medium bowl and whisk them together. Create a well in the centre and add the chilled water, whisking as you do so, to form a smooth batter.

Place a sheet of paper towel on a cooling rack.

Place 5–6 cm (2–2½ in) of neutral oil in a deep saucepan and set over medium-high heat. Check the oil temperature – when you're ready to fry it should be hot enough that a wooden chopstick or wooden spoon sizzles when dipped into the oil.

Coat the fish or mushrooms in the batter, then fry them in the hot oil in batches for 2–3 minutes, turning them frequently until they're an even golden brown all over. Transfer the cooked fish or mushrooms to the lined cooling rack, leaving space between each one so they stay crispy.

Serve hot alongside the other taco fillings and toppings.

# CARNITAS
# (MEXICAN PULLED PORK)

Serves 6

This juicy pulled pork is a staple of any taco night I host! It's the low-maintenance centrepiece that I can cook ahead of time and trust to always be a crowd favourite. It's flavourful and decadent with only a mild chilli flavour, meaning that it's not going to exclude any of your family or friends that struggle with a low spice tolerance. Of course, chilli lovers can add plenty as they assemble their tacos!

1.5 kg (3½ lb) pork shoulder
½ teaspoon garlic powder
½ teaspoon onion powder
1 teaspoon ground cumin
½ teaspoon dried oregano
1 teaspoon smoked paprika
1½ teaspoons soft light brown sugar
1 teaspoon salt
2 onions, sliced
5 garlic cloves, minced
2 fresh jalapeños (or other mild chillies), sliced
2 chipotle peppers in adobo (with sauce, see Note)
500 ml (17 fl oz) pineapple juice, plus extra if needed

Preheat the oven to 160°C Fan (325°F Fan).

Pat the pork shoulder dry with paper towels. If there is any rind on the meat (there likely will be if purchased as a roasting joint) trim it off with a sharp knife. Cut the shoulder into 2 or 3 roughly even pieces.

Combine the garlic and onion powders, cumin, oregano, paprika, sugar and salt in a small bowl, then sprinkle this evenly over all sides of the pork pieces. Place them in a deep, oven-safe lidded pot or casserole dish.

Place the onions, garlic, jalapeños, and chipotle peppers around the pork, then add the pineapple juice. The pork should be 75% submerged, so add a little more juice if needed.

Cover the pot with the lid (or tightly with foil), then place in your oven and cook for 3 hours. Remove the lid and cook for another 25–30 minutes until the liquid has reduced by half.

Shred the pork pieces with forks and allow the meat to rest in the sauce until ready to serve. You can either serve it like this (simply reheat if necessary) or you can crisp it up slightly.

To crisp the meat, heat a frying pan (skillet) over medium-high heat and spread the shredded pork evenly over the surface of the pan. Move the meat around as it fries to get crispy portions throughout, adding some of the braising liquid if necessary to keep it from getting too dry. Serve while hot!

NOTES

*Chipotle peppers in adobo sauce are usually available in supermarkets or Latin-American grocers. I have never seen one that contains gluten but be sure to check the ingredients list! I measure chipotle peppers in adobo sauce in whole chillies as that's how they're stored (usually canned or in a jar) but be sure to include some of the adobo sauce as well.*

*I cook this dish in my oven but you can use a slow cooker or an instant pot if you prefer (refer to the directions of your appliance for the appropriate cooking time for large cuts of meat).*

# FISH SHOP FEAST

The availability of gluten-free options at fish and chip shops seems to be improving all the time, which is great for those of us who love a trip to the seaside. Even when gluten-free battered options are available to us though, I find myself wishing I could order some of the other offerings they have available. I've opted to include some other fried seafood options for those who don't love battered fish, so that you can feel like you're checking out a menu and picking something slightly more exciting or adventurous than the standard fare. These are all delicious, easy ways to eat more seafood, whether you enjoy them as a feast or as stand-alone meals or sides!

# CHIP SHOP CHIPS

Serves 2–3

Cooking fresh chips can be such a hassle. There's a lot of conflicting advice about pre-cooking the potatoes, rinsing versus soaking the cut fries, and then about frying them once, twice or three times for optimal results. Honestly, I just didn't want to have to worry about all that. I wanted an easier way to make yummy, crunchy chips – and I found it! My trick is to use a microwave to pre-cook the potatoes. Then it's a simple matter of frying once to crispy perfection and seasoning as you like. That's it!

2 large, floury/starchy potatoes
neutral oil, for deep frying

**For the chicken salt (optional – see Note)**
1 teaspoon gluten-free chicken powder
¾ teaspoon salt
½ teaspoon caster (superfine) sugar
¼ teaspoon onion powder
¼ teaspoon garlic powder
¼–½ teaspoon dried oregano (optional – not normally in chicken salt but it tastes delicious on these chips)

Use a fork to prick the potatoes 7–8 times all over. Place them on a microwaveable plate and microwave on high (900W) for 5 minutes, then flip the potatoes and repeat. Allow them to cool until cool enough handle.

Meanwhile, if using, make the chicken salt seasoning. Simply combine the ingredients in a bowl or shake together in a jar.

Place 4–5 cm (1½ × 2 in) of oil in a large, deep pan and set over medium heat. Check the oil temperature with a thermometer – when you're ready to fry it should be between 160°C–170°C (320–340°F).

Use a sharp knife to slice the potatoes lengthways into 1 cm (½ in) thick discs. Then slice each disc into 1 cm (½ in) thick batons (do this one disc at a time – the potatoes will be soft, so stacking and cutting won't work). Lay the batons out in a single layer to steam dry and cool a little more, for 4–5 minutes.

Fry the chips in batches to avoid overcrowding the pan. Cook for 4–5 minutes, stirring regularly, until they're golden and crunchy. Transfer to a wire rack while you cook the rest.

Place the cooked chips in a large bowl and add the chicken salt (or your preferred seasoning), then toss to coat before serving.

NOTE

*I've included a recipe for my homemade chicken salt because it's an absolute staple back home in Australia but not so common elsewhere. Of course, you can opt to go for just salt (and vinegar – yum), but you won't be sorry if you decide to give my chicken salt a go! If you want to make a bigger batch, simply double or triple the quantities and store it in a jar.*

# BEER-BATTERED SNAPPER

Serves 2–3

Snapper is generally my go-to for fish and chips but feel free to substitute your favourite white fish for this recipe – they all work well in this batter. The important thing is to use fresh fish, rather than frozen, if possible, as frozen fish tends to retain a lot of moisture, which can prevent the batter from staying crisp.

neutral oil, for deep-frying
2–3 snapper fillets (about 300 g/10½ oz) per fillet)

**For the beer batter**
50 g (1¾ oz) rice flour
100 g (3½ oz) gluten-free cornflour (cornstarch)
20 g (⅔ oz) chickpea (gram) flour
¾ teaspoon salt
¼ teaspoon gluten-free baking powder
150 ml (5 fl oz) chilled gluten-free beer

To make the batter, combine all the dry ingredients in a mixing bowl, then add the beer and mix until smooth. Set aside for 5–10 minutes, then briefly mix again.

Place 5–6 cm (2–2½ in) of oil in a large, deep saucepan and set over medium heat. Check the oil temperature – when you're ready to fry it should be hot enough that a wooden chopstick or wooden spoon sizzles when dipped into the oil.

Pat the fish fillets dry with paper towels. To coat, rather than dipping the fish into the batter and moving it around, lay a fillet in the bowl of batter and use your fingers to 'lift' batter to coat the top side of the fish. This will be easier than trying to move delicate fish around in the thick batter.

When the fish fillet is fully coated in a thick layer of batter, transfer it quickly but carefully into the hot oil. Fry the fish for 2–3 minutes, turning it a few times as it cooks to ensure it cooks evenly, until it is crisp and golden brown. Transfer to a wire rack to drain while you cook the remaining fillets.

Serve piping hot, with lemon wedges, tartare sauce. mushy peas and a side of chips (page 172).

NOTES

*The texture of this batter is atypical because of the high ratio of cornflour, but that's what makes it so deliciously crunchy. It will be a little stiff to mix at first but, if you keep mixing gently, it will relax into a nice, thick batter.*

*Drain the fried fish on a wire rack to keep it as crisp as possible.*

# POTATO SCALLOPS

Serves 2–3

Potato scallops or potato cakes? I'm pretty sure they're just different names for the same thing – thin slices of potato, coated in batter and deep-fried. I use the same method here as I do for my chip shop chips (page 172) – the microwave! This saves the hassle of pre-cooking the potato and ensures a tender middle with a crispy golden crust.

2 large, floury/starchy potatoes
1 quantity of **beer batter** (page 174)
neutral oil, for deep frying
salt

Use a fork to prick the potatoes 7–8 times all over. Place them on a microwaveable plate and microwave on high (900W) for 3 minutes, then flip the potatoes and repeat. Allow them to cool until cool enough handle.

Meanwhile, make the beer batter according to the instructions on page 174.

Place 4–5 cm (1½–2 in) of oil in a large, deep pan and set over medium heat. Check the oil temperature with a thermometer – when you're ready to fry it should be between 210°C–220°C (410–430°F).

As the oil heats, prepare the potato scallops. Use a sharp knife to slice the potatoes lengthways into 0.5–1 cm (¼–½ in) thick discs. Lay these out in a single layer to steam dry and cool a little more for 4–5 minutes.

Coat the potato slices in the batter. Rather than dipping them into the batter and moving them around, lay them in the bowl of batter and use your fingers to 'lift' batter to coat the top side of the potato slices. This will be easier than trying to move the partially cooked potatoes around in the mixture.

When the potato slices are fully coated in a thick layer of batter, transfer them quickly but carefully into the hot oil (being careful not to overcrowd the pan – fry in batches if necessary). Fry the potato scallops for 4–5 minutes, turning them a few times as they cook to ensure they brown evenly. When they are crisp, slightly puffy and golden brown, transfer them to a wire rack to drain.

Serve while piping hot sprinkled with salt.

# CHILLI CRUMBED CALAMARI

Serves 2–3

**Whether it's salt and pepper squid or lemon pepper squid, I think some kind of floured or crumbed calamari is definitely a staple for many a fish shop feast, especially back home in Australia. I've made these my own with some added flavour and spice, but they're still reminiscent of calamari served at plenty of fish and chip shops, pubs and cafés If squid is your go-to order, I highly recommend you give these a go. You can always adjust the spice level to your taste!**

50 g (1¾ oz) rice flour
2 eggs
250 g (9 oz) fresh squid rings (or squid tubes cut into 1 cm/½ in rings)
neutral oil, for deep frying
gluten-free Kewpie mayonnaise and sweet chilli sauce, to serve (optional)

**For the coating**
100 g (3½ oz) gluten-free coarse/panko breadcrumbs (fresh or shop-bought)
½ teaspoon salt
⅛ teaspoon white pepper
1 tablespoon gochugaru (coarse Korean chilli flakes) (or 1 teaspoon chilli powder)
2 tablespoons white sesame seeds
½ teaspoon onion powder
½ teaspoon garlic powder

Place all the coating ingredients in a medium bowl, mix well and set aside. Place the rice flour in a second bowl; beat the eggs in a third bowl.

Working with one or two squid rings at a time, dip them first into the flour to coat on all sides, then into the beaten eggs. Make sure they're well coated, then toss them in the coating mixture. Apply some pressure to ensure they're completely coated, then lay them on a plate or tray in a single layer until ready to cook.

Place 4–5 cm (1½–2 in) of oil in a large, deep pan and set over medium heat. Check the oil temperature – when you're ready to fry it should be between 160°C–170°C (320–340°F); hot enough that a wooden chopstick or wooden spoon sizzles when dipped into the oil.

In batches, fry the coated squid rings for about 3 minutes, turning them occasionally to ensure they brown evenly, until golden and crisp. Transfer them to a wire rack while you cook the rest.

Serve while piping hot with Kewpie mayo and sweet chilli sauce for dipping, if using.

# SWEET AND SPICY COCONUT PRAWNS

Serves 2–3

These obviously don't appear on the average fish and chip shop menu, but they're a delicious way to eat prawns nonetheless! The crispy coating with coconut makes them beautifully fragrant and, when combined with the pineapple flavour of the sauce, they're like a slightly spicy, tropical treat. I recommend eating them as they are, but they're also incredible as the protein in small sliders as well – which I think would get snapped up immediately at a barbecue lunch on the beach.

50 g (1¾ oz) rice flour
¼ teaspoon salt
2 eggs
60 g (2¼ oz) gluten-free fine breadcrumbs (fresh or store-bought)
20 g (¾ oz) desiccated (dried shredded) coconut
250 g (9 oz) prawns (shrimp), peeled (tail left on) and deveined
neutral oil, for frying
sesame seeds, to serve

**For the sauce**
1 teaspoon sesame oil
1 teaspoon grated fresh ginger
2 garlic cloves, minced
2–3 tablespoons runny honey (adjust to taste)
1 tablespoon gluten-free gochujang paste (or hot sauce of choice)
150 ml (5 fl oz) pineapple juice
1 tablespoon gluten-free cornflour (cornstarch) mixed with 2 tablespoons water to form a slurry
⅛–¼ teaspoon salt (to taste)

To make the sauce, heat the sesame oil, ginger and garlic in a small saucepan over low–medium heat until fragrant. Add the honey and gochujang and stir well to combine, then pour in the pineapple juice and bring to a simmer. When simmering, whisk in the cornflour slurry and cook until the sauce has thickened and there is no floury taste. Season to taste with salt, then remove from the heat and set aside.

Grabs three small bowls. Combine the rice flour and salt in the first bowl; beat the eggs in the second bowl; mix the breadcrumbs and coconut in the third bowl.

Holding each prawn by its tail, first dredge the prawns in the flour mixture to coat, then dunk them in the egg, and finally coat with the breadcrumbs and coconut, ensuring they are completely and tightly coated all over (except the tail).

Place 1 cm (½ in) of neutral oil in a deep frying pan (skillet) and set over medium heat. Check the oil temperature – when you're ready to fry it should be hot enough that a wooden chopstick or wooden spoon sizzles when dipped into the oil.

Fry the prawns in batches for 1–2 minutes on one side, then turn and fry for a further 1 minute until golden on both sides. Transfer the cooked prawns to a wire rack while you fry the rest.

Sprinkle the prawns with sesame seeds, then either serve drizzled with the sauce, or with the sauce on the side as a dip.

# PINEAPPLE FRITTER

Serves 4–6

I'm an advocate of using fresh pineapple to make fritters (rather than canned slices), largely because fresh pineapple has so much more flavour. Of course, canned pineapple can be easier to get hold of, so if that's all you can find, go for it. Just be sure to dry each slice with paper towels as much as possible before cooking, as the moisture from the fruit can prevent the batter from staying crisp. I like to serve mine with a dusting of icing sugar or vanilla sugar for a little extra sweetness.

1 fresh pineapple (or 2 × 272 g/9½ oz cans pineapple slices, drained and dried)
1 quantity of **beer batter** (page 174)
neutral oil, for deep frying
icing (powdered) sugar or vanilla sugar, to serve

Trim the top and bottom off the pineapple, then cut away the skin. Turn it on its side, cut it into 1 cm (½ in) slices, then use a small cookie cutter (or carefully use a sharp knife) to remove the core from each slice. Lay the slices on plenty of paper towels, then top with some more, to drain away excess moisture.

Prepare the beer batter according to the instructions on page 174.

Place 4–5 cm (1½–2 in) of oil in a large, deep pan and set over medium heat. Check the oil temperature – when you're ready to fry it should be between 160°C–170°C (320–340°F); hot enough that a wooden chopstick or wooden spoon sizzles when dipped into the oil.

Coat the pineapple slices in the batter. Rather than dipping them into the batter and moving them around, lay them in the bowl of batter and use your fingers to 'lift' the batter to coat the top side of the pineapple slices. This will be easier than trying to move them around in the mixture.

When the pineapple slices are fully coated in a thick layer of batter, transfer them quickly but carefully into the hot oil (be careful not to overcrowd the pan – fry them one at a time if necessary). Fry for 3–4 minutes, turning them a few times as they cook to ensure they brown evenly, until crisp, slightly puffy and golden brown. Transfer them to a wire rack to drain while you cook the rest.

Dust with icing sugar or vanilla sugar and serve while piping hot!

# TAKE OUT FEAST

Growing up, going to the local Chinese restaurant
was my all-time favourite treat. So much so, it became
a bit of a running joke in the family.

'What do you want for your birthday dinner?
Let me guess … Chinese?'

Every time, without fail. And I haven't changed.

This meant that my coeliac disease diagnosis was a pretty big blow!
Luckily, over the years, I've learnt to cook all the classics so that
I don't feel like I'm missing out on anything. These aren't
necessarily traditional recipes, but they are dishes typically
found in every neighbourhood Chinese restaurant in Australia
(and, I've discovered, in the UK, too)! I hope that making
and eating these meals brings you all the comfort and
nostalgia that they give me.

# EGG FRIED RICE

Serves 4

This is a really easy fried rice that goes well with any of the dishes in this feast (although for a mid-week meal option, steamed rice is also perfectly fine!). Think of it as a bit of a blank canvas and feel free to add your favourite vegetables or protein if you like. I tend to use fried rice as a bit of a fridge cleanout option, adding any small amounts of vegetables I happen to have on hand. You can also add leftover roast meats, ham, bacon or prawns if you have some – add these with the spring onion, garlic and ginger to impart the most flavour and you'll have a delicious rice dish that can be whipped up in less than 20 minutes.

4 eggs
3 tablespoons vegetable oil
3–4 spring onions (scallions), finely sliced
4–5 garlic cloves, minced
2–3 cm (1 in) piece of fresh ginger, peeled and grated
600 g (21 oz) cooked jasmine rice (cooked weight)
½ teaspoon gluten-free chicken powder (or ¼ teaspoon salt)
¼ teaspoon caster (superfine) sugar
1 tablespoon gluten-free soy sauce
2½ tablespoons gluten-free oyster sauce
1 tablespoon sesame oil
salt and white pepper

Crack the eggs into a mixing bowl, add ⅛ teaspoon of white pepper and ¼ teaspoon of salt and whisk well. Set aside.

Place a large wok or frying pan (skillet) over high heat and add 2 tablespoons of vegetable oil, along with the spring onions, garlic and ginger. Stir fry until fragrant, then add the rice. Mix well to break up any clumps of rice but avoid constant stirring – you want to allow the rice to catch slightly to provide texture and a little smokiness.

When the rice is heated through, push it to the side of the pan. Add the remaining 1 tablespoon of oil to the pan, then add the beaten eggs. Allow them to cook, agitating them a little as needed, until the eggs are about 80% cooked. Combine the rice with the egg and toss vigorously to combine.

Add the chicken powder, sugar, soy sauce, oyster sauce, sesame oil and ¼ teaspoon of white pepper and continue to toss and stir constantly to disperse the flavours throughout the rice. Cook for another minute or two, then serve while piping hot.

### NOTE

*I recommend you use rice that has been pre-cooked, preferably a day in advance and then refrigerated overnight, or store-bought microwaveable rice. This will give the best texture and flavour. However, if it is most convenient for you to use freshly cooked rice, that's perfectly fine.*

pictured on page 194

# SALT AND PEPPER PRAWNS

Serves 4

The aromatics in this dish work beautifully with the crispy prawns, but you can easily swap the prawns for other proteins, like squid or chicken. You can also make a vegan version with enoki mushrooms – pull them into bite-sized bunches and then follow the recipe below (leave off the marinade as this makes the mushrooms soggy).

neutral oil, for frying
2 spring onions (scallions), finely sliced

**For the prawns**
300 g (10½ oz) prawns (shrimp), peeled and deveined
1 teaspoon gluten-free soy sauce
1 teaspoon gluten-free oyster sauce
1 teaspoon sesame oil
¼ teaspoon bicarbonate of soda (baking soda)
1 tablespoon gluten-free cornflour (cornstarch)
¼ teaspoon white pepper

**For the salt and pepper mix**
1 tablespoon neutral oil
2 garlic cloves, finely chopped
2 shallots, finely chopped
2 red or green chillies, finely sliced
2 dried Szechuan chillies
½ teaspoon caster (superfine) sugar
¼ teaspoon white pepper
¼–½ teaspoon salt, to taste

**For the batter**
30 g (1 oz) **basic flour blend** (page 18)
60 g (2 oz) gluten-free cornflour (cornstarch)
½ teaspoon salt
¼ teaspoon white pepper
¼ teaspoon gluten-free baking powder
120 ml (4 fl oz) water, chilled
1 teaspoon gluten-free Shaoxing rice wine (or other rice wine)

Start by marinating the prawns. Place them in a small bowl and add the rest of the ingredients. Mix well and set aside.

Next, make the salt and pepper mix. In a large wok or frying pan (skillet), heat the neutral oil over medium heat and add the garlic, shallots and fresh and dried chillies. Stir fry until cooked through, then add the sugar, white pepper and salt. Toss to combine, then turn off the heat.

Fill a medium saucepan approximately one-third full with neutral oil and place over medium-high heat. Check the oil temperature – when you're ready to fry it should be hot enough that a wooden chopstick or wooden spoon sizzles when dipped into the oil.

For the batter, place the dry ingredients in a medium bowl and whisk to combine. Create a well in the centre and pour in the chilled water and rice wine. Whisk until a smooth batter has formed.

Working in batches, coat about 3 prawns in the batter, then lower them into the hot oil. Fry for 2–3 minutes, turning them regularly to encourage even browning. Use a slotted spoon to transfer them to a cooling rack while you coat and cook the rest of the prawns.

Once all the prawns are cooked, place the wok with the salt and pepper mix back over high heat until sizzling. Add the fried prawns and spring onions, then toss briefly to combine and coat everything with the seasonings. Transfer to a serving dish and serve immediately.

pictured overleaf

# HONEY CHICKEN

### Serves 4

I don't know about you, but no matter who I'm dining with at a Chinese restaurant, the eventual appearance of honey chicken at the table is basically an inevitability. It's a family favourite (for good reason) and my version of this crunchy, sweet, tender chicken dish tastes exactly like you'd expect from your local, except maybe a smidge better? Because it comes with the security of knowing that you're definitely not about to get 'glutened'!

neutral oil, for frying
50 g (1¾ oz) dried rice vermicelli (optional)
toasted sesame seeds, to serve

**For the chicken**
400 g (14 oz) skinless chicken breast fillets or tenders
¼ teaspoon salt
¼ teaspoon white pepper
¼ teaspoon caster (superfine) sugar
1 teaspoon gluten-free Shaoxing rice wine (or other rice wine)
¼ teaspoon bicarbonate of soda (baking soda)
½ teaspoon sesame oil
2 tablespoons gluten-free cornflour (cornstarch)

**For the sauce**
90 ml (3 fl oz) runny honey
45 ml (1½ fl oz) cold water
1½ teaspoons caster (superfine) sugar
¼ teaspoon salt

**For the batter**
30 g (1 oz) **basic flour blend** (page 18)
60 g (2 oz) gluten-free cornflour (cornstarch)
½ teaspoon salt
¼ teaspoon white pepper
¼ teaspoon gluten-free baking powder
120 ml (4 fl oz) water, chilled
1 teaspoon gluten-free Shaoxing rice wine (or other rice wine)

To prepare the chicken, trim away any excess fat, then slice against the grain into bite size pieces (about 3–4 cm/1¼–1½ in). Place the chicken pieces in a bowl along with all the other ingredients and use your hand to massage the marinade into the chicken, making sure each piece is well-coated. Cover the bowl with cling film (plastic wrap) and refrigerate for 20 minutes.

Meanwhile, to make the sauce, measure all the ingredients into a small saucepan and set it over medium heat. Heat until the sugar and salt have just dissolved, then remove from the heat and set the saucepan aside. Don't transfer the sauce to a serving dish yet, as it'll be reheated on the stove immediately before serving.

Fill a large, deep saucepan about one-third full with neutral oil and set it over medium-high heat. Check the oil temperature – when you're ready to fry it should be hot enough that a wooden chopstick or wooden spoon sizzles when dipped into the oil.

For the batter, place the dry ingredients into a medium bowl and whisk to combine. Create a well in the centre and pour in the chilled water and rice wine, whisking constantly, until you have a smooth batter.

If using, break up the dried vermicelli noodles a little by hand, then carefully drop them into the hot oil. They will cook and puff up almost immediately so have a kitchen spider or slotted spoon ready to scoop them out. Transfer them to a cooling rack to drain away any excess oil.

Now fry the chicken. Working with 5–6 pieces of chicken at a time, transfer them from the marinade to the bowl of batter, ensuring each piece is well coated. Carefully lower the coated chicken into the hot oil and fry in batches for 3–4 minutes, turning them regularly to encourage even browning. Transfer to the cooling rack.

While the last batch of chicken is cooking, place the honey sauce back over low heat and bring to a simmer. Transfer the crispy noodles onto a serving platter, then either toss the cooked chicken pieces in the sauce or place the chicken directly onto the plate and drizzle the sauce over the top. Sprinkle with sesame seeds and serve immediately.

# SWEET AND SOUR PORK

Serves 4

I've been making versions of this recipe for years but have only recently discovered how to *perfect* it! And it's using a technique that is popular in Chinese cooking but which can also level up many other dishes. It's called velveting, which is a marinating technique that helps to tenderise meat and keep it moist throughout the cooking process. There are various iterations and no universal recipe, but I have settled on a combination of ingredients that yields perfect results every time. The key is bicarbonate of soda (baking soda in the US – not to be confused with baking powder). By including a small amount of bicarbonate of soda in the marinade, you can make any meat incredibly succulent and flavourful. I do this in stir fries as well as fried dishes like this sweet and sour pork or my honey chicken (page 196), and the result is incredible! By having such tender meat inside a thin, crispy batter, you really get the best of everything in terms of taste and texture.

neutral oil, for frying

**For the pork**
400 g (14 oz) pork loin steak
¼ teaspoon salt
¼ teaspoon white pepper
¼ teaspoon caster (superfine) sugar
1 teaspoon gluten-free Shaoxing rice wine (or other rice wine)
¼ teaspoon bicarbonate of soda (baking soda)
½ teaspoon sesame oil
1 tablespoon gluten-free cornflour (cornstarch)

**For the sweet and sour sauce**
½ tablespoon vegetable oil
½ onion, roughly chopped
1 small carrot, peeled and roughly chopped
1 small red (bell) pepper, deseeded and roughly chopped
125 ml (4¼ fl oz) cold water
3 tablespoons rice vinegar
3 tablespoons tomato ketchup
3 tablespoons caster (superfine) sugar
1 tablespoon runny honey
¼ teaspoon salt, plus extra to taste
150 g (5½ oz) fresh pineapple pieces
1 tablespoon gluten-free cornflour (cornstarch) mixed with 2 tablespoons water to form a slurry

**For the batter**
30 g (1 oz) **basic flour blend** (page 18)
60 g (2 oz) gluten-free cornflour (cornstarch)
½ teaspoon salt
¼ teaspoon white pepper
¼ teaspoon gluten-free baking powder
120 ml (4 fl oz) water, chilled
1 teaspoon gluten-free Shaoxing rice wine (or other rice wine)

To prepare the pork, trim away any excess fat, then slice into 2–3 cm (1 in) pieces. Place the pork pieces in a bowl along with all the other ingredients and use your hand to massage the marinade into the meat, making sure each piece is well-coated. Cover the bowl with cling film (plastic wrap) and refrigerate for 20–30 minutes.

...continues overleaf

In the meantime, prepare the sauce. Add the oil to a medium saucepan set over medium heat, then add the onion, carrot and red pepper. Cook for 2–3 minutes, stirring regularly, until the carrots just start to soften, then add the rest of the sauce ingredients (except for the pineapple and cornflour slurry). Bring to a simmer. When the vegetables are tender, add the pineapple and the cornflour slurry. Stir to combine and allow the sauce to cook and thicken for another minute, or until the pineapple has heated through and there is no floury taste in the sauce. Set the saucepan aside.

Fill a large, deep saucepan about one-third full with neutral oil and set it over medium-high heat. Check the oil temperature – when you're ready to fry it should be hot enough that a wooden chopstick or wooden spoon sizzles when dipped into the oil.

For the batter, place the dry ingredients in a medium bowl and whisk to combine. Create a well in the centre and pour in the chilled water and rice wine, whisking constantly, until you have a smooth batter.

Working with a handful of pork pieces at a time, transfer them from the marinade to the bowl of batter, ensuring each piece is well coated. Carefully lower the coated pork into the hot oil and fry in batches for 4 minutes, turning them regularly to encourage even browning. Transfer to the cooling rack.

While the last batch of pork is cooking, place the sweet and sour sauce back over low heat and bring to a simmer. Working quite quickly, transfer the cooked, crunchy pork pieces to the saucepan and toss briefly to coat them evenly in sauce. Tip the pork, sauce and vegetables onto a platter and serve immediately.

# PRAWN TOAST

### Serves 6–8

I had actually never tried prawn toast before my coeliac diagnosis. I was lucky enough to find a Chinese restaurant that offered a gluten-free version though and I've been hooked ever since. It's now one of my favourite savoury bites and, if you like prawns, I think you're going to love it, too! My version is a little more aromatic than what might be typical but I promise, it is absolutely delicious.

280 g (10 oz) prawns (shrimp), peeled and deveined
1–2 garlic cloves, finely chopped
½ teaspoon grated fresh ginger
1 spring onion (scallion), green and white parts separated, both finely sliced
¼ teaspoon white pepper
½ teaspoon caster (superfine) sugar
½ teaspoon gluten-free chicken powder (or ¼ teaspoon salt)
½ teaspoon gluten-free soy sauce
1 teaspoon sesame oil
1 tablespoon gluten-free cornflour (cornstarch)
6 slices of gluten-free white bread (see page 118 for homemade)
40 g (1½ oz) white sesame seeds
neutral oil, for frying

Weigh out 200 g (7 oz) of the prawns and chop them very finely to create a mince. Transfer to a medium bowl, then roughly chop the remaining prawns into 1–2 cm (½–¾ in) pieces. Add these to the bowl along with the garlic, ginger and sliced white part of the spring onion.

Add the pepper, sugar, chicken powder, soy sauce, sesame oil and cornflour, then mix well until it resembles a rough paste. Divide the mixture between the slices of bread, using a spatula to spread it in an even layer right to the edges of each slice. Compact the prawn mixture onto bread by applying gentle pressure as you spread it.

Place the sesame seeds in a shallow bowl larger than the bread slices, then one by one, place each slice prawn side-down into the sesame seeds. Move the bread around a little to make sure that all the prawn mixture is covered by a layer of sesame seeds.

Place 2–3 cm (1 in) neutral oil in a deep frying pan (skillet) and set over medium heat. Check the oil temperature – when you're ready to fry it should be hot enough that a wooden chopstick or wooden spoon sizzles when dipped into the oil.

Working with two or three bread slices at a time (or as many as will fit in the pan), carefully place each one prawn side-down into the hot oil. Fry for about 2 minutes before carefully flipping each piece and frying for a further 2 minutes. The bread should be a rich, golden brown colour and crisp all over. Transfer to a cooling rack to drain away any excess oil and repeat with the remaining slices.

Garnish the prawn toast with the spring onion greens and serve while hot.

pictured on page 194

# EGG NOODLES

### Serves 3–4

These are the egg noodles I serve with my chicken chow mein (overleaf). They crisp up beautifully when fried so that when topped with the saucy stir fry, they basically rehydrate with the sauce to take on all the delicious flavour. As much as I know it's a little tiresome to make your own noodles, I feel the flavour, novelty and experience is well worth it! It's also a fantastic skill to have up your sleeve as a gluten-free cook, as making doughs like this opens the door to all kinds of dumplings and noodles, or even pastry (the phyllo pastry in my first book *The Very Hungry Coeliac* uses a similar technique, for example). These egg noodles are also a great option for noodle soups and other stir-fries so there's ample reason to make them!

50 g (1¾ oz) rice flour, plus extra for dusting
35 g (1¼ oz) gluten-free cornflour (cornstarch)
35 g (1¼ oz) tapioca starch
25 g (1 oz) glutinous rice flour
2 teaspoons xanthan gum
2 teaspoons psyllium husk powder
2 eggs
2 teaspoons neutral oil
40–60 ml (about 3–4 tablespoons) boiling water

Weigh the dry ingredients into a food processor or the bowl of your stand mixer. You can also mix the noodles by hand, but the mixing/kneading takes longer.

Crack the eggs into a separate jug, add the oil, then whisk lightly to combine.

Pour the egg mixture into the dry ingredients, whisking constantly, until it is well-dispersed through the flour mix. Then, still while mixing, trickle in the boiling water. Start with about 40 ml (just under 3 tablespoons) and then pause to see how well the dough is coming together (the size of the eggs can affect the amount of water needed, as well as slight variations in the absorbency of the starches). Continue adding small amounts of boiling water until the dough comes together in a slightly tacky ball, cleaning the side of the bowl or the food processor. Gather the dough in your hands and roll it into a smooth log.

Lightly flour a clean work surface with rice flour and rolling out the dough to 0.5–1 cm (¼–⅜ in) thick. At this stage you can roll the dough through a pasta machine/roller until it is 1 mm (¹⁄₁₆ in) thick (the 5th or 6th setting on a pasta roller), or simply keep using the rolling pin to roll by hand. As you roll, dust the dough with more rice flour to prevent it sticking. When properly rolled, it should feel like a sheet of cloth and be flexible enough to fold and crumple without tearing.

Once thin enough, dust the dough with more rice flour, roll it into a flattish log, then use a sharp knife to trim off the ends and cut it into thin noodles. You can also cut it using the pasta cutting attachment on your roller or stand mixer (the 'angel hair' cutter is best). The noodles should be as thin as possible so that they fry quite quickly and crisp nicely.

Once cut, shake out the noodles to remove any excess rice flour then shape into nests and set aside in an airtight container or covered bowl until cooking. If making them in advance, store in the fridge.

# CHICKEN CHOW MEIN
# (WITH CRISPY EGG NOODLES)

Serves 4

I have vivid memories of the time when this dish was my favourite on any Chinese restaurant menu; it was my go-to if I was allowed a special treat after a Saturday morning netball game. In fact, I remember I used to check my fixtures and look forward to the games that would finish during the hours when our local Chinese offered their special lunch deals, because I knew I'd get the opportunity to cajole a celebratory (or commiserating) lunch out of my mum. I make my own gluten-free egg noodles (page 202) but, if you prefer, you can serve this with fried rice noodles instead, which won't be exactly like what you remember from your local restaurant but will hit the spot with less hassle. To do so, follow the instructions for frying the noodles that I serve with my honey chicken on page 197.

neutral oil, for frying
1 quantity of **egg noodles** (page 202)
2 tablespoons vegetable oil
1 onion, sliced
1 red (bell) pepper, deseeded and sliced
1 large carrot, peeled and sliced
2–3 cm (1 in) piece of fresh ginger, peeled and finely chopped
3–4 garlic cloves, finely chopped
2–3 heads of bok choy, stems and leaves separated, both cut into chunks
½ broccoli, cut into florets
6–8 button mushrooms, sliced
5–6 baby corn spears, halved lengthways
2–3 spring onions (scallions), chopped into 5 cm (2 in) pieces

**For the chicken**
1 skinless chicken breast
¼ teaspoon salt
¼ teaspoon white pepper
¼ teaspoon caster (superfine) sugar
¼ teaspoon bicarbonate of soda (baking soda)
1 teaspoon gluten-free Shaoxing rice wine (or other rice wine)
1 teaspoon gluten-free soy sauce
1 teaspoon sesame oil
1 tablespoon gluten-free cornflour (cornstarch)

**For the sauce**
1 tablespoon gluten-free Shaoxing rice wine (or other rice wine)
1 tablespoon gluten-free soy sauce
1 tablespoon gluten-free oyster sauce
1 teaspoon sesame oil
500 ml (17 fl oz) hot chicken stock
1 tablespoon gluten-free cornflour (cornstarch) mixed with 2 tablespoons water to form a slurry

Start by preparing the chicken. Trim off any excess fat, then slice against the grain into thin slices. Place in a bowl with the rest of the ingredients, then use your hand to massage the marinade into the chicken, making sure each piece is well-coated. Cover the bowl with cling film (plastic wrap) and refrigerate for 20–30 minutes.

Combine the ingredients for the sauce (except the stock and cornflour slurry) in a bowl and mix well. Set aside.

...continues overleaf

Place 3–4 cm (1¼–1½ in) of neutral oil in a large, deep saucepan and set over medium-high heat. Check the oil temperature – when you're ready to fry it should be hot enough that a wooden chopstick or wooden spoon sizzles when dipped into the oil.

Working quickly but carefully, drop the nests of egg noodles in an even layer around the pan. Try not to agitate them much while cooking as they will become crispy and brittle quite quickly. Fry the noodles for about 2 minutes, then flip the nests as best you can. Fry for a further 2 minutes, or until the nests are crisp all the way through, then use a kitchen spider or slotted spoon to remove them from the pan and onto a cooling rack.

Place a large wok or frying pan (skillet) over high heat. Add the vegetable oil and swirl it around the wok. When the oil is hot, add the chicken, spreading it in a single layer around the base of the wok. Allow to sear before starting to toss to cook on all sides. When the chicken is 90% cooked (some undercooked spots are fine as the chicken will be cooked again at the end), transfer it to a bowl, leaving any excess oil in the wok.

Add the onion, red pepper and carrot to the pan, and cook for a minute or so, stirring and tossing regularly. Add the ginger, garlic, bok choy stems, broccoli, mushrooms and corn and toss to combine. Cook for another minute or two, then add the remaining vegetables, as well as the chicken, sauce mixture and chicken stock. Stir until everything is well combined, then add the cornflour slurry and stir well until the sauce has thickened and the vegetables and chicken are cooked (the vegetables should still have a slight bite to them).

Place the crispy noodle nests in a large serving bowl, then pour the stir-fry on top, making sure to spread the sauce out evenly over the noodles. Serve immediately!

# BEEF AND BLACK BEAN SAUCE

Serves 3–4

Making this beef and black bean stir-fry will likely necessitate a trip to an Asian grocer to track down the fermented black beans, also known as salted black beans or *douchi*. These are black beans that have been fermented in salt and they're a delicious, umami-packed addition to many Chinese dishes. I like to soak mine in rice wine, preferably Shaoxing or mijiu, but sake will also do in a pinch as the aforementioned options can be hard to track down when hunting for gluten-free options (read more about gluten-free cooking wines on page 12). Don't worry if you can't find the beans though, because even without them, this is a delicious stir-fry in its own right. Simply follow the recipe, leaving out the beans but using the rice wine as listed, and then season with salt to taste before serving.

2 tablespoons vegetable oil
2–3 dried Szechuan chillies (optional)
1 onion, roughly chopped
1 red (bell) pepper, deseeded and roughly chopped
1 small carrot, peeled and sliced
2–3 cm (1 in) piece of fresh ginger, peeled and finely chopped
3–4 garlic cloves
½ broccoli, cut into florets
2–3 spring onions (scallions), chopped into 5 cm (2 in) pieces

**For the beef**
300 g (10½ oz) beef rump steak
½ teaspoon caster (superfine) sugar
¼ teaspoon bicarbonate of soda (baking soda)
⅛ teaspoon salt
¼ teaspoon white pepper
1 teaspoon gluten-free soy sauce
1 teaspoon gluten-free Shaoxing or other rice wine
1 teaspoon sesame oil
1½ tablespoons gluten-free cornflour (cornstarch)

**For the sauce**
4 tablespoons fermented black beans
50 ml (1⅔ fl oz) gluten-free Shaoxing rice wine (or other rice wine)
1 tablespoon gluten-free oyster sauce
1½ tablespoons gluten-free hoisin sauce
½ tablespoon sesame oil
100 ml (3⅓ fl oz) cold water

...continues overleaf

Start by preparing the beef. Trim off any excess fat or gristle, then slice against the grain into thin slices. Place in a bowl and add the rest of the ingredients, then use your hands to massage the marinade into the meat, making sure each piece is well-coated. Cover the bowl with cling film (plastic wrap) and refrigerate for 20–30 minutes.

Now prepare the sauce. Place the fermented black beans in a fine mesh sieve and rinse well under cold running water. Transfer them to a small bowl and add the Shaoxing rice wine, then use a fork to rough mash about half of them. Set aside to soak for 10–15 minutes. Place the rest of the sauce ingredients into another bowl and mix well to combine, then set aside.

Now you can stir fry. Place a large wok or frying pan (skillet) over high heat. Add the vegetable oil and swirl it around the pan. When the oil is hot, add the beef, spreading it in a single layer around the base of the wok. Allow it to sear well before starting to toss to cook on all sides. When the beef is 70–80% cooked (some undercooked spots are fine as the beef will be cooked again at the end), transfer the beef to a bowl, leaving any excess oil in the wok.

If using, add the dried chillies to the pan and allow them to get darker in colour for about 1 minute, then add the onion, red pepper and carrot, and cook for another 1 minute, stirring and tossing regularly. Add the garlic, ginger and broccoli and toss to combine.

Add the black bean/Shaoxing mixture and toss well to coat all the vegetables. Allow to cook for 2–3 minutes, stirring and tossing regularly, until the vegetables are slightly tender (they should still have a bite to them). Now add the beef back to the pan along with the remaining sauce ingredients. Toss well to combine and cook for another minute before adding the spring onions.

Once the spring onions have wilted and the vegetables are cooked through (still a little crunchy), transfer the stir-fry to a large dish and serve immediately.

# WINTER WARMER FEAST

Wintery days call for hearty, warming dishes and, for me, that has always meant spices. Not necessarily chilli (although I do love a kick of heat), but spices that provide lots of complex flavour and warm you up from the inside out. There's something for everyone in this feast – whether it's the crispy bhajis, the silky potato-stuffed momo, or the sweet, super-rich pudding I've included for dessert. In my opinion, the really special recipe here though is the garlic naan! It's something I've been working on for a long time so be sure to give it a go, not just to have with this feast but to use as a flat bread or side wherever you need to mop up a tasty sauce.

# GARLIC NAAN

Makes 8

I'm so excited about this recipe. I've been working on a pan-fried flat bread on and off for years, but it's been difficult to create something that was soft and pliable that also cooks relatively quickly in a pan. Gluten-free starches often benefit from longer cooking times in the oven, as they hydrate very differently to wheat flour and require more time for internal moisture to evaporate. In saying that, these are *perfect*. Of course, working with yeast is a little tricky if you're not familiar with it, so I recommend reading some of the hints I've included on page 36 before you get started, to make sure you get the best, most delicious naan possible!

280 g (9¼ oz) warm water (37–40°C/100–105°F is ideal)
1 tablespoon instant dried yeast
2 tablespoons caster (superfine) sugar
160 g (5⅔ oz) **basic flour blend** (page 18), plus extra for dusting
120 g (4¼ oz) rice flour
4 teaspoons psyllium husk powder
1 teaspoon xanthan gum
1 tablespoon gluten-free baking powder
½ teaspoon salt
2 teaspoons apple cider vinegar
1 tablespoon lard, chilled
vegetable oil, for greasing

### For the garlic butter
40 g (1½ oz) unsalted butter, melted
4 garlic cloves, minced
¼ teaspoon salt
1 tablespoon finely chopped coriander (cilantro) leaves (optional)

Add the warm water to a medium jug or bowl, then mix in the yeast and 1 tablespoon of the sugar. Cover and leave in a warm, draft-free place for 10 minutes until the yeast has 'bloomed', which means there is a thick layer of foam on the surface. (If a layer of foam has not formed, your yeast may not be active and the naans will not work properly. See page 36 for guidance on working with yeast.)

Meanwhile, combine the flours, psyllium husk, xanthan gum, baking powder, salt and the remaining 1 tablespoon of sugar in a large mixing bowl or the bowl of a stand mixer.

Add the vinegar to the yeast mixture, then pour this into the dry ingredients. Mix slowly (with the paddle attachment if using a mixer) until mostly combined, then mix vigorously (medium speed on a mixer) for 4–5 minutes, scraping down the side of the bowl once or twice to ensure all the ingredients are combining.

When the dough is smooth (it will still be quite wet and sticky), add the lard and continue mixing until no lumps of lard remain.

Grease a large bowl with the vegetable oil, then transfer and gather the dough into it. Shake and rotate the bowl a little to ensure the dough is a uniform ball, then flip it over. The aim is to have a smooth ball of dough that is greased all over, not to incorporate more fat into the dough, so try to avoid handling it and dimpling the dough with your fingers. Cover the bowl with cling film (plastic wrap) and place in a warm, draft-free place for 1 hour.

...continues overleaf

Dust your work surface with a little of the basic flour blend, then tip the dough out and dust that with flour, too. Knead the dough by hand for 30–40 seconds, removing the air bubbles until it is smooth.

Divide the dough into 8 even pieces then, working with one piece at a time, roll them out into an oval shapes, just less than 0.5 cm (¼ in) thick. Dust with flour as necessary to prevent the dough from sticking. They will puff up during their second prove, then again while cooking, so do not be tempted to leave the dough thicker at this stage.

As you roll out the naan, stack them on sheets of baking paper to prevent them from sticking together. Once all have been rolled, cover with a tea towel (dish towel) and leave to prove in a warm, draft-free place for 20 minutes until doubled in size and puffy.

Heat a large frying pan (skillet) over medium–low heat (do not add oil). When the pan is hot, very gently transfer as many naans as will fit into the dry pan (it may just be one, that's fine) and cook for 5–6 minutes on one side, or until they have puffed on top and developed golden brown patches on the side in contact with the pan. Flip and cook for a further 5–6 minutes on the other side. Use a spatula to gently press down on the naan if they puff, to help them brown evenly. Once cooked, transfer to a wire rack to cool completely – do not be tempted to skip this step; the naan need to cool initially to help set the crumb as this stops them from becoming gummy.

While the naans cool, prepare the garlic butter by combing all the ingredients in a small bowl.

When the naan have cooled completely, heat a large frying pan over high heat. Place the naan breads in a single layer in the pan and cook quickly on both sides, just long enough to heat them through, not long enough to toast them (you may have to do this in batches).

Remove them from the pan and brush liberally with the garlic butter. They're now ready to serve!

# ONION BHAJIS

Makes 10–12

These are the perfect crispy side to serve before or with a meal. Especially if you're not quite finished cooking when your family or friends get to the table. No-one is going to complain when there's a plate of these to snack on while they wait. They're very mildly spiced but still packed with flavour. And the natural sweetness from the onions is just so delectable with the light, crispy batter.

4 onions, finely sliced
1 teaspoon fine salt
1 teaspoon ground coriander
2 teaspoons curry powder
½ teaspoon ground turmeric
6 tablespoons chickpea (gram) flour
2 tablespoons rice flour
½ teaspoon gluten-free baking powder
neutral oil, for frying
1–2 tablespoons cold water (if needed)
flaky salt
**mint raita** (opposite), to serve

Place the onions in a large mixing bowl along with the salt and spices, then massage the seasonings into the onions by hand. Start gently at first, then as the onions soften start squeezing with more pressure as you massage them. Set them aside for 5 minutes to allow the salt to draw more moisture out of the onions.

In a separate small bowl, combine the chickpea flour, rice flour and baking powder.

Give the onions another mix, again massaging by hand until they are quite wet, then add the flour mixture and mix well. The flour should combine with the moisture from the onions to create a tacky batter.

Add 2 cm (1 in) oil to a deep frying pan (skillet), then set the pan over medium-high heat for 2–3 minutes.

Give the onions another mix. If there is not enough batter to clump the onion slices together, add 1–2 tablespoons of water and mix well. Take a small handful of onion and place in a single pile in the oil. You can use a spoon to shape the pile lightly into a clump, but do not compress it or it won't be light and crispy when cooked.

Repeat with more of the onions but don't overcrowd the pan. Cook for 3–4 minutes on each side, then transfer to a cooling rack.

Sprinkle the bhajis with flaky salt and serve hot with mint raita on the side for dipping.

# MINT RAITA

Serves 4–6

**This simple, herbaceous mint sauce is delicious, especially when dunking onion bhajis (opposite) or my garlic naan (page 213). It's just what you need to cool down when serving up a delicious, spicy feast.**

15 g (½ oz) mint leaves
5 g (¼ oz) coriander (cilantro) leaves
⅛ teaspoon ground cumin
¼ teaspoon caster (superfine) sugar (or to taste)
¼ teaspoon salt (or to taste)
1 teaspoon lime juice
1 green chilli (optional)
130 g (4½ oz) plain Greek-style yogurt

Place all ingredients in a blender and blend until smooth and bright green. The raita is ready to serve immediately but you can also store it in the fridge until use. It will thicken slightly as it chills.

# COCONUT RICE

Serves 4–6

**This rice has a mild sweetness from the coconut milk that combines with the warmth of cardamom and cinnamon to perfectly complement any curry.**

360 g (12½ oz) basmati rice
400 ml (14 oz) can coconut milk
600 ml (20 fl oz) cold water
¼ teaspoon salt
3 cardamom pods
1 cinnamon stick

Wash the rice in running water until the water runs clear (or very nearly so). Place it in a large saucepan and add the coconut milk, water, salt, cardamom pods and cinnamon stick.

Place the saucepan over high heat and bring to a gentle boil, then cover with a lid and reduce the heat to low. Allow to cook for 15 minutes. Do not stir it at any point during cooking.

After 15 minutes, turn off the heat and allow to stand with the lid on for another 10 minutes before fluffing with a fork and serving.

# CHICKEN CURRY

Serves 4–6

**This curry is a distillation of lots of different curries I've made over the years, and it's become a favourite to have on really windy, rainy days because it's hearty, warming and easy to make. It's also made with all my favourite spices, so I've almost always got all the ingredients ready in my pantry. Feel free to adjust the chilli level to your taste. You can also customise this a little, depending on whether you prefer a straight tomato base or something a little creamier, which is why I add a small amount of yogurt. I suggest serving this with coconut rice (page 217) and my garlic naan (page 213) so you can mop up all the sauce!**

3 tablespoons ghee
2 cinnamon sticks
5–6 cardamon pods
2 teaspoons black mustard seeds
2 teaspoons cumin seeds
7–8 garlic cloves, minced
2 tablespoons grated fresh ginger
6 shallots, finely sliced
1 green chilli, halved (optional)
2 teaspoons ground coriander
2 tablespoons curry powder
1 teaspoon ground cumin
½ teaspoon chilli powder
500 g (18 oz) boneless, skinless chicken thighs, chopped into bite-sized pieces
2 × 400 g (14 oz) cans chopped tomatoes
250 ml (8½ fl oz) cold water
½ teaspoon caster (superfine) sugar
small handful of coriander (cilantro), chopped (optional)
2–3 tablespoons plain Greek-style yogurt (optional)
salt

Heat the ghee gently in a wok or large, deep frying pan (skillet). Add the cinnamon sticks and cardamom pods and cook for about 1 minute until the cardamom pods start to swell.

Add the mustard and cumin seeds and fry for 30–40 seconds; they should be fragrant and sizzling in the ghee. Add the garlic and ginger and cook for 10–20 seconds, then add the shallots, chilli (if using) and ½ teaspoon of salt. Cook for about 3 minutes until the shallots have softened and are translucent.

Add the all the ground spices and cook for 20–30 seconds, until fragrant, then add the chicken. Fry just long enough to seal the meat, then add the tomatoes and water.

Stir and bring to a simmer, then reduce for 5–10 minutes, stirring regularly until the curry has thickened and the chicken is cooked through. Taste and add the sugar and more salt if needed. If using, stir in the coriander and yogurt, then remove from the heat and serve.

# POTATO MOMO AND CHILLI TOMATO CHUTNEY

Makes about 30

'Momo' are South Asian dumplings and the first time I had them was in Nepal (in my pre-coeliac days). They're so hearty and comforting when stuffed full of spiced potato and the chutney is absolutely *packed* with flavour. The combination of the spicy elements with the fragrance of roasted tomatoes, aromatics and coriander in the chutney will fill a hole in your gluten-free heart that you didn't even know was there!

1 quantity of **dumpling wrappers** (page 52)
small handful of coriander (cilantro), roughly chopped, to serve
salt and cracked black pepper

**For the filling**
2 large floury/starchy potatoes, peeled and chopped
2 teaspoons ghee or vegetable oil
2 shallots, finely chopped
3 garlic cloves, minced
2 teaspoons grated fresh ginger
1 green chilli, deseeded and finely chopped (optional)
½ teaspoon garam masala
1–2 tablespoons finely chopped coriander (cilantro)

**For the chutney**
3 medium tomatoes
1–3 red chillies (omit or adjust to taste)
3 teaspoons grated fresh ginger
3 garlic cloves
15 g (½ oz) coriander (cilantro)
1 tablespoon vegetable oil
½ teaspoon rice vinegar
½ teaspoon caster (superfine) sugar

First make the filling. Place the potatoes in a pot of cold, well-salted water and bring to the boil. Cook until fork tender, then drain and mash them roughly with a fork.

Meanwhile, in a frying pan (skillet), heat the ghee and cook the shallots, garlic, ginger, and chilli until softened. Add the garam masala and cook until fragrant, then add this to the mashed potatoes. Season with salt and pepper to taste and stir in the coriander.

To fold the dumplings, place a small spoonful of the filling into the centre of a wrapper. Lightly moisten your finger with water and run it over one side of the wrapper. It should become slightly sticky. (If it's wet and slippery, you've used too much water. Simply let it dry slightly before folding and/or dust your fingertips with tapioca starch or rice flour to prevent the wrapper from getting soggy.) Fold the wrapper in half over the filling and press the dry side onto the moistened side to seal. You can pleat as you go or leave it as a simple semi-circle. Repeat with the rest of the filling and wrappers, then place them into lined steamer baskets (or arrange them on plates lightly dusted with rice flour if storing to cook later).

Steam the dumplings for 10–12 minutes over medium-high heat.

While they cook, make the chutney. Char the tomatoes and chillies (if using) on a wire rack set over your stovetop. Direct contact with a flame is best but you can also grill (broil) them to achieve a similar result. Transfer the charred veg to a bowl, cover with cling film (plastic wrap) and allow to sit for 5 minutes. Remove the worst of the charred skin, then place the tomatoes and chillies in a blender or food processor, along with the ginger, garlic and coriander. Blitz a rough sauce.

In a small saucepan, heat the oil, then add the chutney mixture. Bring to a simmer, then reduce for about 5 minutes. Season with the vinegar, sugar and salt to taste, then transfer to a serving dish and place the hot momo on top, garnished with coriander to serve.

# STICKY CARROT PUDDING WITH SPICED BUTTERSCOTCH

Serves 6–8

I love this pudding because it perfectly combines two of my all-time favourite sweet treats – carrot cake and sticky date or sticky toffee pudding. It was actually initially inspired by a traditional North Indian dessert called halwa, which is made by cooking grated carrots in milk with sugar and some mild spices to form a pudding, which is then served with toasted nuts. All three desserts are delicious, so I think it goes without saying that this recipe follows suit!

180 g (6⅔ oz) soft light brown sugar
120 g (4¼ oz) unsalted butter, plus extra for greasing
2 eggs
80 g (2¾ oz) ground almonds
40 g (1½ oz) **basic flour blend** (page 18)
50 g (1¾ oz) rice flour
1½ teaspoons gluten-free baking powder
½ teaspoon salt
1 teaspoon ground cinnamon
½ teaspoon ground cardamom
50 ml (1⅔ fl oz) milk
200 g (7 oz) carrot, grated (about 3 medium carrots)
thick double (heavy) cream, to serve

**For the butterscotch sauce**
100 g (3½ oz) soft light brown sugar
100 g (3½ oz) unsalted butter
60 ml (2 fl oz) single (light) cream
¼ teaspoon salt, plus extra to taste
¼ teaspoon ground cinnamon
¼ teaspoon ground cardamom

Preheat the oven to 170°C Fan (340°F Fan) and grease a 16 × 24 cm (6 × 9½ in) baking dish with butter. Set aside.

In a large bowl, cream together the sugar and butter with a hand-held electric beater. When light and fluffy, add the eggs one at a time, beating well in between each addition.

Sift together the dry ingredients, then fold them into the creamed mixture. Add the milk and stir until smooth, then add the grated carrot and mix it through the batter.

Transfer the batter to the prepared baking dish, smoothing it out into an even layer. Bake for 55–60 minutes, until a skewer inserted into the centre comes out clean (with only moist crumbs attached – no wet batter).

As it bakes, make the butterscotch sauce. Combine the sugar and butter in a small saucepan and set it over medium heat. Allow the butter to melt and sugar to dissolve, stirring with a spatula. When fully combined, add the single cream, salt and spices, and mix well.

When the pudding is cooked through, allow it to cool for 15–20 minutes. Reheat the sauce if necessary, then transfer it to a pouring jug. Serve big spoonfuls of the pudding with a generous drizzle of the sauce and some double cream.

# CELEBRATION FEAST

Major holidays are always a wonderful time for family gatherings and food, but it can be a source of a lot of anxiety for people with coeliac disease or gluten intolerance. After all, where there's food, there's potential risk of getting sick, and there's nothing worse than this happening over a holiday period that should be about joy and relaxation. In my family, large holiday celebrations usually involve some kind of roast dinner with *lots* of trimmings – luckily, this is something that can easily be made gluten free. The recipes in this collection will hopefully give you plenty of options and ideas for making a massive, celebratory gluten-free meal that *everyone* will be able to enjoy!

# ROASTIES WITH PARMESAN + HERBS

Serves 4–6

**Potatoes that are pillowy on the inside, crisp on the outside, with loads of flavour from garlic, herbs and Parmesan cheese. What's not to love?**

1–1.5 kg (about 3 lb) small–medium potatoes (skin-on)
4 garlic cloves, minced
2 tablespoons rosemary leaves, finely chopped (or 2 teaspoons dried)
1 tablespoon thyme leaves, finely chopped (or 1½ teaspoons dried)
75 g (2¾ oz) Parmesan, grated
6 tablespoons extra virgin olive oil
1–2 teaspoons flaky salt

Place the potatoes in a large pan of cold, salted water and bring to the boil. Boil until a skewer can slide easily through the potato (15–20 minutes), then drain and set aside to steam-dry for 5–10 minutes.

Preheat the oven to 180°C Fan (350°F Fan).

Combine the garlic, herbs, Parmesan and 4 tablespoons of the olive oil in a medium bowl and mix well. Spread this mixture into a roasting tray.

Slice the cooked potatoes in half lengthways and place them cut-side-down onto the herb and Parmesan mixture. Drizzle with the remaining 2 tablespoons of olive oil and season with the salt.

Roast the potatoes for 30–35 minutes, or until the cheese layer has browned, then remove from the oven. Allow to cool for 5–10 minutes to allow the cheese to crisp up, then transfer the potatoes to a platter and serve.

# PORK BELLY ROAST WITH APPLE + FENNEL STUFFING

Serves 4–6

This is a crowd-pleasing roast that's made a little fancy to give it an extra celebratory kick. The stuffing comes together quickly and adds so much flavour to the pork. It also absorbs a lot of moisture as the roast cooks, so the stuffing itself is moist and completely delicious!

boneless pork belly joint (about 1.5 kg/3½ lb)
2 teaspoons Dijon mustard
2–3 teaspoons vegetable oil
flaky salt and cracked black pepper
gluten-free gravy, to serve

### For the stuffing
1 shallot, finely chopped
3 garlic cloves, minced
1 apple, peeled, cored and finely diced
½ fennel bulb, finely diced
1 tablespoon rosemary leaves, finely chopped (or 1 teaspoon dried)
1 teaspoon thyme leaves, finely chopped (or ½ teaspoon dried)
3–4 sage leaves, finely chopped (or ½ teaspoon dried)
1 teaspoon oregano leaves, finely chopped (or ½ teaspoon dried)
2 slices of gluten-free bread, finely chopped (see page 118 for homemade)
3 tablespoons extra virgin olive oil

During the morning on the day of roasting, remove the pork belly from any packaging (take note of the weight of the meat as this will affect the cook time). Score the skin with a sharp knife, pat it dry with paper towel and place it on a rack set over a roasting tin. Sprinkle it generously with 2–3 teaspoons of salt, then refrigerate uncovered for several hours.

Combine all the ingredients for the stuffing in a bowl and season well with salt and pepper.

Remove the pork from the refrigerator and allow it sit at room temperature for about 1 hour before you begin cooking (this should be 3–4 hours before you plan to serve).

Preheat the oven to 220°C Fan (425°F Fan).

Scrape away the salt you applied earlier, then use paper towel to wipe away any remaining moisture from the skin. On a dry board, lay 3–4 lengths of kitchen twine horizontally in front of you, spaced about 4 cm (1½ in) apart. Then place the pork belly skin side-down on top of them, with a long side closest to you.

Brush the mustard in a light layer over the exposed meat, then add the stuffing mixture in a log shape along the centre of the meat, spreading a little of the stuffing to the edges of the pork, too. Compact the stuffing into the meat with your hands.

Bring the ends of the pork belly together to encase the stuffing and use the twine to tie the meat closed (this will be easier if someone helps to tie as you hold the pork belly in place). Tie as tightly as possible and use more twine if needed to ensure it's secure. Turn the roast over so it is seam side-down and place back on the (clean) rack set over a roasting tin.

...continues overleaf

Brush the skin all over with a little vegetable oil and then season well with salt. Place in the centre of your oven and cook for 35–40 minutes until the skin has crackled. Then reduce the oven to 180°C (350°F) and cook for a further 30 minutes per 500g (just over 1 lb).

When the pork is ready, remove it from the oven and allow it to rest for 10 minutes before carving and serving. Serve with your favourite gluten-free gravy and sides.

NOTE

*You can chop the stuffing ingredients by hand if needed, but I use a food processor for ease as everything needs to be finely chopped to produce a stuffing mixture that will hold together when squeezed between your hands.*

# YORKSHIRE PUDDINGS

Makes 12

I'm going to level with you – growing up, Yorkshire puddings were never a staple with my roast dinners. My mum was never a fan and in Australia they don't have quite the cult following they have in the UK. Spending a lot of time *in* Yorkshire made me realise they must be something special so I set to work creating a recipe that would make me reconsider my opinion of them. After a lot of trial and error, I've settled on these beauties. These days, they're not only always on the table with a roast, but they're absolutely devoured and no matter how many I make, we somehow never have leftovers.

Adding some oregano to the batter (please bear with me, Brits) and cooking them in lard or tallow gives them a little extra aroma that really makes them taste like a roast all the way through, so by the time you add gravy, each mouthful is like a mini roast appetiser.

20 g (⅔ oz) **basic flour blend** (page 18)
70 g (2½ oz) gluten-free cornflour (cornstarch)
¼ teaspoon gluten-free baking powder
¼ teaspoon salt
¼ teaspoon dried oregano
3 eggs (about 165 g/5¾ oz total shelled weight)
140 ml (5 fl oz) milk
about 100 g (3½ oz) lard or beef tallow (or shortening for a vegetarian option)

Preheat the oven to 220°C Fan (425°F Fan).

In a mixing bowl, whisk the dry ingredients together, then create a well in the centre. Add the eggs and whisk well to make a smooth, thick batter. Add the milk and whisk again until smooth. Set the batter aside to rest for 10–15 minutes.

Meanwhile, divide the lard between the holes of a 12-hole muffin tray. Aim for 7–8 g (1 heaped teaspoon) in each hole. When the oven is hot, place the tray in the oven for 5 minutes to melt the lard and bring it over 200°C (400°F).

Transfer the batter to a jug (pitcher) for easy pouring. Working quickly, take the muffin tray out of the oven (close the oven door to retain the heat) and pour the batter evenly into the holes of the muffin tray (there should be enough batter to fill each muffin hole approximately one-third full). Quickly but carefully place the tray back in the oven. Bake for 16–20 minutes (see Note).

When cooked to your liking, remove from the oven and allow to cool for 2–3 minutes. You can transfer them to a wire rack to drain away any excess fat or simply serve them directly from the muffin tray.

NOTE

*When baking these, 18 minutes is the sweet spot in my oven. This forms an excellent, crispy crust that I love and a thin layer of stretchy softness throughout the hollow in the centre. If you prefer them a little softer, cook for 1–2 minutes less; if you want them even more crisp and crunchy, cook for 1–2 minutes more!*

# ROASTED FENNEL WITH PANGRATTATO

Serves 4–6

As someone who absolutely cannot tolerate liquorice, it has taken me some time to be swayed by fennel. Saying that, I have always appreciated the subtle sweetness it can bring to savoury meals, which is why I like to add some fennel to the stuffing of my roasts or to soup stocks. Roasting fennel to have as a side dish is therefore a relatively new obsession, but I cook it in a way that brings out all the sweetness and aroma, while dulling some of the aniseed flavour, and find it pairs beautifully with so many meals. While the fennel is incredibly succulent and tender, the pangrattato on top provides a delicious, perfectly seasoned crunch.

2 fennel bulbs
250 ml (8½ fl oz) vegetable stock (or stock of your choice)
2 teaspoons extra virgin olive oil

**For the pangrattato**
2 garlic cloves
1 teaspoon thyme leaves
½ teaspoon lemon zest
2 slices of gluten-free bread, torn (or 60 g/2¼ oz gluten-free panko breadcrumbs)
20 g (¾ oz) Parmesan, finely grated
flaky salt and cracked black pepper

Preheat the oven to 180°C Fan (350°F Fan).

Remove and discard the tough stems and any discoloured outer layers from the fennel bulbs. Now quarter each bulb and trim away any exposed core. Place the fennel quarters in a casserole or roasting dish.

Add the stock, then drizzle over the olive oil. Cover the dish with foil and bake for 30 minutes, then remove the foil, flip the fennel pieces, and bake for a further 20 minutes.

Meanwhile, make the pangrattato. Place the garlic cloves, thyme and lemon zest into a food processor and blitz until finely chopped. Add the bread and blitz again until you have a rough crumb. (If you're using breadcrumbs, you can chop the garlic and thyme by hand and mix all the ingredients in a bowl.) Stir in the Parmesan, then season generously with salt and pepper.

Once the fennel has been cooking for 50 minutes, flip the pieces again and top each one generously with the pangrattato mixture. Return to the oven to cook for a final 15–20 minutes, until the pangrattato is golden brown and the fennel is juicy and tender.

# HONEYED CARROTS WITH CARAWAY SEEDS

Serves 4–6

Caraway seeds are aromatic and slightly bittersweet, sort of like peppery citrus. I don't see them served with carrots a lot but it's one of my favourite vegetable flavour pairings, especially when sweetened with a little honey. These carrots come out tender and delicious, so they're a great veggie side dish to whip up when you want extra flavour with minimal effort!

500 g (about 1 lb) carrots, peeled and halved lengthways
60 ml (2 fl oz) water
2 tablespoons honey
15 g (1 tablespoon) unsalted butter
½ teaspoon flaky salt
¼ teaspoon caraway seeds

Preheat the oven to 180°C Fan (350°F Fan).

Place the carrots in a baking dish and add the remaining ingredients. Toss well, ensuring the honey and seasonings coat the carrots.

Roast for 45–50 minutes, turning halfway through cooking, or until the carrots are tender and caramelised. Serve while hot.

# CHARRED GREENS WITH BUTTER + LEMON

Serves 4–6

I love to serve roasts with a side of vivid greens to lighten things up a little; you might be surprised how tasty they can be with a knob of butter and a squeeze of lemon. Don't feel you're limited to serving these with roast meats, either. I do my greens like this to complement many meals, sometimes adding some creamy feta cheese and toasted nuts (like pine nuts or flaked almonds) to make them into a more substantial meal.

300 g (10½ oz) tenderstem broccoli, tough ends trimmed
150 g (1½ oz) green beans, trimmed
1 tablespoon extra virgin olive oil
1 tablespoon unsalted butter
2 teaspoons lemon juice
flaky salt

Bring a large pot of salted water to the boil. Half fill a large bowl with ice cubes and cold water.

Blanch the broccoli and green beans for 30–40 seconds, then transfer them to the iced water. Once cool, transfer the vegetables to a board and pat them dry with paper towel.

Set a large frying pan (skillet) over high heat and add the oil. When hot, spread the vegetables around the pan. Cook for 30–40 seconds, or until there are some charred patches, then flip them and reduce the heat to low.

Add the butter, lemon juice, and salt to taste and toss to disperse through the vegetables. When the butter is melted and the vegetables are cooked through (they should still have a slight bite), transfer them to a platter to serve.

NOTE

*When baking these, 18 minutes is the sweet spot in my oven. This forms an excellent, crispy crust that I love and a thin layer of stretchy softness throughout the hollow in the centre. If you prefer them a little softer, cook for 1–2 minutes less; if you want them even more crisp and crunchy, cook for 1–2 minutes more!*

# TIRAMISU

Serves 6–8

I love a good tiramisu for so many reasons – it's obviously incredibly rich and delicious, but it's also pretty straightforward to make and can be prepped ahead of time, meaning that it's ideal for entertaining. You can of course buy ready-made gluten-free ladyfingers (also known as savoiardi), if you can find them, to make this recipe even simpler, but they can be very expensive and hard to come by so I just make my own.

4 egg yolks
⅛ teaspoon salt
1 teaspoon vanilla bean paste (or extract)
160 g (5⅔ oz) caster (superfine) sugar
500 g (18 oz) mascarpone
2 egg whites
120 ml (4 fl oz) espresso or strong black coffee
1–2 tablespoons Kahlúa, Frangelico, Baileys, whiskey or rum, to taste (optional)
2 teaspoons unsweetened cocoa powder

**For the ladyfingers**
3 eggs, separated
¾ teaspoon vanilla bean paste (or extract)
105 g (3¼ oz) caster (superfine) sugar
90 g (3 oz) superfine rice flour
30 g (1 oz) gluten-free cornflour (cornstarch)
¼ teaspoon xanthan gum
¾ teaspoon gluten-free baking powder
⅛ teaspoon salt
3 tablespoons icing (powdered) sugar

Start by making the ladyfingers. Preheat the oven to 180°C Fan (350°F Fan) and line two baking sheets with baking paper.

Place the egg yolks in a large bowl (you can also use a stand mixer) along with the vanilla and roughly half the caster sugar. Beat with an electric hand whisk until thick, creamy and very pale (it should be almost white in colour). Set aside and clean the whisk/beaters.

Place the egg whites in another bowl along with the remaining caster sugar and beat with an electric hand whisk (or stand mixer) until thick, glossy and able to hold medium-stiff peaks.

Briefly beat the egg yolk mixture again, then add about one-third of the whites mixture to the yolk mixture and gently fold it in, maintaining as much air as possible. Fold the remaining whites mixture into the yolk mixture in two batches.

When nearly combined, sift in the remaining dry ingredients (except for the icing sugar) and gently fold them into the batter. You shouldn't have lumps of dry ingredients but there will be air in the mixture, preventing it from appearing smooth.

Transfer the mixture to a piping bag or large sandwich bag and cut a 1–2 cm (½–¼ in) hole in the end. Pipe the mixture onto the prepared trays in lines that are about 10–12 cm (4–4¾ in) in length and 3–4 cm (1¼–1½ in) wide, leaving 2–3 cm (¾–1¼ in) between each. Sift the icing sugar over the ladyfingers to generously and evenly cover them (use a little more or less than stated to achieve an even coating).

...continues overleaf

Bake for 16–18 minutes until they're golden and crisp. Allow them to cool on the baking sheet for 10–15 minutes, then transfer to a rack to cool completely.

When the ladyfingers are cool, you can make and assemble the tiramisu. Start by placing the egg yolks, salt, vanilla and about two-thirds of the caster sugar into a large mixing bowl. Beat with an electric hand whisk until thick, creamy and very pale (it should be almost white in colour). Mix in the mascarpone until fully combined, then set aside and clean the whisk/beaters.

In another bowl, whisk the egg whites until thick, glossy and able to hold medium-stiff peaks. Gently fold this into the mascarpone mixture until combined.

Pour the coffee into a shallow bowl wide enough to fit a ladyfinger and, if using, stir in your chosen liquor. Place a casserole or baking dish (about 16 × 24 cm/6¼ × 9½ in) next to the dish containing the coffee. One at a time, quickly submerge the ladyfingers in the coffee and then transfer them to the dish. Each biscuit should be covered in the coffee but don't dunk for longer than a second or so, or they will become soggy. Line the base of the dish with coffee-soaked ladyfingers, breaking or cutting them as needed to get one even layer.

Spoon about half the mascarpone mixture onto the ladyfingers and smooth it out, making sure it fills any gaps between or around the biscuits.

Repeat the coffee dunking with another layer of ladyfingers, laying them over the mascarpone layer. Top with the remaining mascarpone mixture, smoothing it out and pushing it into any gaps around the ladyfingers.

Using a sieve, dust an even layer of cocoa powder over the top of the tiramisu. Place the tiramisu in the fridge for at least 3–4 hours before serving.

### NOTE

*This is a traditional-style tiramisu, in that it includes raw eggs. This is something you might not be familiar with, but please don't let that turn you off. I am quite sensitive to any sort of 'eggy' taste, and I assure you, this has none of that. It's just fluffy, creamy and ever so custardy in the best way.*

# PANETTONE

Serves 6–8

I'm so excited to share a panettone recipe with you as it's another thing that I used to think was beyond the realm of possibility! If you haven't had panettone before, it's a traditional Italian baked treat with a really interesting texture – somewhere between cake and a light brioche bread. It's shaped a little like a cake as well, as the dough is typically cooked in a panettone mould, that is, a sturdy paper case that looks like a giant cupcake case. As the dough bakes, it rises into a tall loaf that then peaks over the top of the mould. It is then usually cut into wedges or slices, just as you would serve a birthday cake. The dough is flavoured with dried fruit and lots of citrus, so the result is a buttery, soft, very aromatic and delicately sweetened bread.

**For the fruit mix**
60 g (2¼ oz) fine mixed dried fruit
30 g (1 oz) candied citrus rind (or substitute with extra fine mixed dried fruit)
1½ tablespoons orange zest
2 teaspoons lemon zest
2 tablespoons runny honey
1 teaspoon apple cider vinegar
2 teaspoons vanilla bean paste (or extract)

**For the dough**
190 g (6¾ oz) warm water (37–40°C/100–105°F is ideal)
4 teaspoons instant dried yeast
2 tablespoons caster (superfine) sugar, plus an extra 1 teaspoon
330 g (11½ oz) **basic flour blend** (page 18), plus extra for dusting
4 teaspoons psyllium husk powder
2 teaspoons xanthan gum
1 tablespoon gluten-free baking powder
1¼ teaspoons salt
2 eggs, plus 2 egg yolks
120 g (4¼ oz) unsalted butter, chilled and cubed
vegetable oil, for greasing

**For the egg wash and to finish**
1 egg yolk
2 tablespoons single (light) cream
knob of unsalted butter (about 10 g/⅓ oz), chilled
icing (powdered) sugar, for dusting (optional)

First prepare the fruit mix. In a small bowl, combine the mixed dried fruit, candied citrus and orange and lemon zest. Mix in the honey, vinegar and vanilla, then set aside.

Now move on to the dough. Add the warm water to a medium jug or bowl, then mix in the yeast and 2 tablespoons of caster sugar. Cover and leave in a warm, draft-free place for 10 minutes until the yeast has 'bloomed', which means there is a thick layer of foam on the surface. (If a layer of foam has not formed, your yeast may not be active and the panettone will not work properly. See page 36 for guidance on working with yeast.)

Meanwhile, combine the flour, psyllium, xanthan gum, baking powder, salt and the extra 1 teaspoon of caster sugar in the bowl of a stand mixer.

Beat the eggs and extra egg yolks into the yeast mixture, then pour this into the dry ingredients. Add the fruit mix. Stir gently (with the paddle attachment) until mostly combined, then mix vigorously (medium speed on a mixer) for 4–5 minutes, scraping down the side of the bowl once or twice to ensure all the ingredients are combining. When the dough is smooth (it will still be quite wet and sticky), add the cubed butter then run the mixer until no lumps of butter remain.

In a stand mixer on medium speed, expect to mix the dough for a total of 8–9 minutes. If doing things by hand, you will need to mix vigorously for 12–15 minutes (this is necessary to make the dough as elastic as possible).

Grease a large bowl with the vegetable oil, then transfer and gather the dough into it. Shake and rotate the bowl a little to ensure the dough is a uniform ball, then flip it over. The aim is to have a smooth ball of dough that is greased all over, not to incorporate more fat into the dough, so try to avoid handling it and dimpling the dough with your fingers. Cover the bowl with cling film (plastic wrap), then a tea towel (dish towel), and place it in a warm, draft-free place for 1 hour.

Prepare the cake pan, if using (see Note, overleaf) or grab your panettone mould.

Grease your work surface and your hands with some vegetable oil. Tip the dough out and knead the dough by hand for about 1 minute to remove the air bubbles and make it as smooth as possible. It will still be a little sticky so use a dough scraper as necessary to scrape the dough off your work surface. You should be able to gather it into a relatively smooth ball, but it will be a little pockmarked.

Now dust a little flour onto your work surface and the dough. Gently roll the dough around on the flour – you don't want to incorporate any flour into the dough at this stage or create folds or creases in the dough, you simply want to coat the dough ball in a light layer of flour.

Place this gently into the panettone mould (or prepared cake pan), doing your best to avoid damaging the surface of the dough as you do so. Drape cling film over the top of the paper collar, then add a tea towel and leave to prove in a warm, draft-free environment for 20 minutes, or until the dough has doubled in size.

...continues overleaf

Meanwhile, Preheat the oven to 200°C Fan (450°F Fan) and prepare the egg wash by beating together the egg yolk and cream in a small bowl. Grab a small sharp knife or bread lame (for scoring) and the knob of butter.

When the dough has doubled in size, remove the coverings and use a pastry brush to gently coat the panettone with egg wash. Use the knife or bread lame to score a cross across the top of the dough about 1 cm (½ in) deep. Place the knob of butter into the centre of the cross, then place the panettone in the oven.

Bake for 10 minutes, then reduce the oven temperature to 160°C Fan (325°F Fan). Bake for a further 10 minutes, then loosely cover the top of the panettone with foil. Now bake for a further 1 hour 50 minutes until it is a deep golden brown colour but not burnt. Remove from the oven and allow to cool (in the pan if using) for at least 3 hours (this is necessary for the internal crumb to set fully).

Once cooled, you can turn out the panettone and remove the paper collar. I like to dust mine with a little icing sugar, then you can slice and serve immediately.

NOTE

*You will need a 1 kg (2 lb) panettone mould for this recipe. You can also make the panettone in a cake pan but it requires a little fiddling with baking paper. Use a round cake pan that's 16–18 cm (6¼–7 in) in diameter and prepare a sheet of baking paper that is long enough to wrap comfortably around the outside of the pan. Fold the paper in thirds lengthways, so you end up with a long, 3-ply sheet that can line the walls of the cake pan like a tall collar. Do not line or grease the base of the cake pan – you want the dough to stick a little as it bakes to maintain the structure – the dough is buttery enough that once the dough crust has formed and then cooled after baking, you'll be able to easily wiggle it loose. Use a stapler to staple the paper collar closed in 2–3 places where the paper rises above the walls of the cake tin. This is necessary to make sure the panettone rises vertically without busting through the open side of the paper collar.*

# INDEX

## A
alcohol
    Beer-battered snapper 174
    No-churn whiskey butterscotch ice-cream 28
    Tiramisu 241-242
allergens 6-7, 12-13, 16
apples 150, 230
asparagus 117
avocado
    Avocado and lime crema 164

## B
'Baked' beans 30
baking powder 12
Basic flour blend 18
basil 117
Bean curd rolls 76-77
beans
    'Baked' beans 30
    beansprouts 141
    Beef and black bean sauce 207-208
    cannellini beans 30
    green beans 240
    red bean paste 82-83
Beef and black bean sauce 207-208
Beer-battered snapper 174
blueberries
    Blueberry compote 23
    Blueberry frangipane tartlets 105
bok choy 204-206
bread
    Garlic bread (but better) 136
    Garlic naan 213-214
    Prawn toast 201
    Sandwich loaf (or rolls) 118-121
    Spiced fruit loaf 126-127
broccoli 204-208, 240
butterscotch sauce 27-28
button mushrooms 110

## C
cabbage
    green cabbage 147
    red cabbage 141
caraway seeds 238
cashew nuts 116
calamari 181
candied citrus rind 244-247
capers 96
Caramelised onion, mushroom and brie tartlets 110
Carnitas (Mexican pulled pork) 168
carrots
    Ginger and sesame slaw 141
    Honeyed carrots with carraway seeds 238
    Potato + carrot röstis 31
    Sticky carrot pudding with spiced butterscotch 224
char siu bao 78-80
Charred greens with butter + lemon 240
Cheddar and rosemary crackers 114
cheese
    brie 110
    cheddar 114
    cream cheese 129-130, 136
    goats cheese 117
    mascarpone 23, 241-242
Cheeseburger sliders with kimchi slaw 147
cheung fun 62
chicken
    Chicken and shiitake dumplings 60
    Chicken Chow Mein (with crispy egg noodles) 204-206
    Chicken curry 218
    chicken powder 12
    Creamy chicken and bacon pies 112
    Crunchy fried chicken wings 148-149
    Honey chicken 196-197
Chilli crumbed calamari 181
Chip shop chips 172
Chive and pork belly dumplings 58
chocolate
    chocolate buttercream 131-132
    chocolate crème patissiere 99-100
    Chocolate cupcakes with peanut butter caramel 131-132
    cocoa powder 99-100, 131-132, 241-242
    dark chocolate ganache 99-100
    Pain au chocolat 45-47
    S'mores chocolate slice 152-153
choux pastry 96-100
Chunky romesco sauce 116
chutney 222
cilantro SEE coriander
Cinnamon rolls 129-130
cocoa powder 99-100, 131-132, 241-242

coconut
    desiccated coconut 183
    Coconut rice 217
coffee 241-242
coeliac disease 6-7
compote 23, 90
coriander 141, 164, 213-214, 217-218, 222
cornflour (cornstarch) 12, 15-19
courgettes 117
crackers 127
    Cheddar and rosemary crackers 114
craquelin 99-100
cream cheese frosting 129-130
Creamy chicken and bacon pies 112
Crème brûlée tart 103-104
Crispy red bean pancakes 82-83
Crispy waffles 27
Croissants 34-44
Crumpets 24
Crunchy fried chicken wings 148-149
custard 91-92, 103-104

## D

dark chocolate 99-100
dill 96
Double chocolate choux puffs 99-100
dough
    Cinnamon rolls 129-130
    Dumpling wrappers 52-53
    Egg noodles 202
    Flour tortillas 156-178
    Hot cross buns 25-26
    Panettone 244-247
    Puff pastry (the ultimate savoury pastry) 106-109
    Sandwich loaf (or rolls) 118-121
    Scones 88
    Spiced fruit loaf 126-127
    Steamed pork buns take 12 (char siu bao) 78-80
    Wonton wrappers 54-55
    Youtiao (fried Chinese dough) 81-82
dried fruit 25-26, 126-127, 244-247
dumplings
    Chicken and shiitake dumplings 60
    Chive and pork belly dumplings 58
    Dumpling flour blend 19
    Dumpling wrappers 52-53
    Potato momo and chilli tomato chutney 222
    Prawn and pork siu mai 71
    Prawn and scallop har gow 72-73
    Xiao long bao (soup dumplings) 67

## E

Easter 25-26
eggs
    Egg fried rice 190
    Egg noodles 202

## F

fennel
    Pork belly roast with apple + fennel stuffing 230-232
    Roasted fennel with pangrattato 237
fish
    Salmon and dill profiteroles 96-98
    snapper 174
    Spiced battered cod (or mushrooms) 167
flour
    Basic flour blend 18
    cornflour (cornstarch) 12, 15-19
    Dumpling flour blend 19
    Flour tortillas 156-178
    gluten-free flour 14-19
    glutinous rice flour 15-19
    potato starch 15-19
    rice flour 15-19
    sweet potato starch 19
    tapioca starch 15-19
    xanthan gum 15-19
fried rice 190
Fluffy pancakes with mascarpone + blueberry compote 23
fried Chinese dough 81-82

## G

Garlic bread (but better) 136
garlic butter 213-214
Garlic naan 213-214
Ginger and sesame slaw 141
gluten-free ingredients 12-19
glutinous rice flour 15-19
goats cheese 117
gochujang paste 12, 138, 147-149, 183
guacamole SEE Avacado and lime crema
Grilled pineapple salsa 166

## H

Hakka-style stuffed tofu 74
harissa paste 30
honey
    Honey chicken 196-197
    Honeyed carrots with carraway seeds 238
hot chips 172
Hot cross buns 25-26

## I

ice-cream
  No-churn whiskey butterscotch ice-cream 28

## K

kewpie 12
kimchi 147

## L

ladyfingers 241-242
leek 136
leftovers 30
lemon butter 90
lime
Avocado and lime crema 164

## M

Mango pancakes 84
mascarpone 23, 241-242
mayonnaise 12, 96-98, 140-141
  kewpie 12
meatballs 147
meringue 152-153
Mini apple pies 150
Mint raita 217
mushrooms
  Bean curd rolls 76-77
  button mushrooms 110
  Caramelised onion, mushroom and brie tartlets 110
  Chicken and shiitake dumplings 60
  shiitake 60, 76-77

## N

No-churn whiskey butterscotch ice-cream 28
noodles 202-206

## nuts

cashew nuts 116
peanut butter caramel 131-132

## O

onion
  Onion bhajis 216
  Quick pickled red onions 161
oyster sauce 60-67, 72-80, 190-191, 204-208

## P

Pain au chocolat 45-47
pancakes
  Crispy red bean pancakes 82-83
  Fluffy pancakes with mascarpone + blueberry compote 23
  Mango pancakes 84
Panettone 244-247
passata 30
pastries
  Crème brûlée tart 103-104
  Croissants 34-44
  Double chocolate choux puffs 99-100
  Mini apple pies 150
  Pain au chocolat 45-47
  Puff pastry (the ultimate savoury pastry) 106-109
  puff-shortcrust hybrid 109-110, 117
  S'mores chocolate slice 152-153
  Strawberry custard Danishes 91-92
peanut butter caramel 131-132
pie
  Creamy chicken and bacon pies 122
  Mini apple pies 150

Pico de gallo (chunky tomato salsa) 164
pineapple
  Grilled pineapple salsa 166
  Pineapple fritters 186
  pineapple juice 168, 183
  Sweet and sour pork 198-200
pork
  Carnitas (Mexican pulled pork) 168
  Chive and pork belly dumplings 58
  Pork belly roast with apple + fennel stuffing 230-232
  Prawn and pork siu mai 71
  pulled pork 168
  Steamed pork buns take 12 (char siu bao) 78-80
  Sweet and sour pork 198-200
  Sweet spiced pork ribs 138
  Xiao long bao (soup dumplings) 67
potato
  Chip shop chips 172
  Potato + carrot röstis 31
  potato cakes 177
  Potato momo and chilli tomato chutney 222
  Potato scallops 177
  potato starch 15-19
  Roasties with parmesan + herbs 229
  Stir-fried shredded potatoes 68
  sweet potato starch 19
prawns SEE seafood
psyllium husk 16

## R

raspberries
  Raspberry thyme compote 90
red bean paste 82-83
rice flour 15-19

Roasted fennel with pangrattato 237
Roasties with parmesan + herbs 229
rosemary 114, 229-230

## S
S'mores chocolate slice 152-153
Salmon and dill profiteroles 96-98
Salt and pepper prawns 191
Salt and pepper squid tentacles 61
Sandwich loaf (or rolls) 118-121
scallions 31, 61
Scones 88
seafood
   Beer-battered snapper 174
   Chilli crumbed calamari 181
   Hakka-style stuffed tofu 74
   Prawn and pork siu mai 71
   Prawn and scallop har gow 72-73
   Prawn cheung fun 62
   Prawn rolls with roasted garlic mayo 140
   Prawn toast 201
   Salmon and dill profiteroles 96-98
   Salt and pepper prawns 191
   Salt and pepper squid tentacles 61
   Spiced battered cod (or mushrooms) 167
   Sweet and spicy coconut prawns 183
Shaoxing rice wine 12
shrimp SEE seafood
slaw
   Cheeseburger sliders with kimchi slaw 147
   Ginger and sesame slaw 141
   kimchi slaw 147
soup dumplings 67
soy sauce 12
Spiced battered cod (or mushrooms) 167
Spiced fruit loaf 126-127
spring onions (scallions) 31, 61
squid 61, 181
sriracha 138, 148-149
Steamed pork buns take 12 (char siu bao) 78-80
Sticky carrot pudding with spiced butterscotch 224
stir-fry
   Beef and black bean sauce 207-208
   Chicken Chow Mein (with crispy egg noodles) 204-206
   Stir-fried shredded potatoes 68
   Sweet and sour pork 198-200
strawberries
   Strawberry custard Danishes 91-92
stuffing 230-232
Summer vegetable tart 117
Sweet and spicy coconut prawns 183
Sweet and sour pork 198-200
sweet potato starch 19
Sweet spiced pork ribs 138

## T
tapioca starch 15-19
tart
   Blueberry frangipane tartlets 105
   Caramelised onion, mushroom and brie tartlets 110
   Crème brûlée tart 103-104
   custard tart 103-104
   Summer vegetable tart 117
thyme 90, 110, 122, 229-230, 237
Tiramisu 241-242
tomato
   canned chopped tomatoes 218
   Chilli tomato chutney 222
   Chunky romesco sauce 116
   Pico de gallo (chunky tomato salsa) 164
   tomato passata 30
tortillas 156-158
tofu
   Bean curd rolls 76-77
   silken tofu 74
   tofu skin sheets 76

## V
Vanilla mascarpone 23

## W
waffles
   Crispy waffles 27
water chestnuts 72-73, 76-77
Whipped lemon butter 90
whiskey 28
wontons
   Wonton wrappers 56-57

## X
xanthan gum 15-19
Xiao long bao (soup dumplings) 67

## Y
yeast 36
Yorkshire puddings 233
Youtiao (fried Chinese dough) 81-82
Yum Cha 51

## Z
zucchini 117

# ACKNOWLEDGEMENTS

As with any major project, there is a large group of people that have helped to bring this book to life. First and foremost, to my partner – thank you for brainstorming with me, for tasting and eating many iterations of each recipe, and of course, for being brutally honest when necessary! You're always nothing but supportive, even when the kitchen is in a diabolical state from a full day of recipe tests.

A big thank you to my family and friends. I consider myself ridiculously lucky to have such amazing people in my life, cheering on from all sides. I love that I have a team of dedicated, gluten-eating recipe testers to make sure that my food always hits the mark.

Of course, to Simon and the team at Hardie Grant, thank you for being excited by my recipes. And thank you for seeing the gluten-free community and being willing to get this book to them.

The editorial and creative team that have worked so hard to bring this book to life also need very special acknowledgement. Harriet, you're an editorial wizard. Thank you for holding my hand through this process and making this book the best it could be. I have a tendency to blab but you have a way of cutting it back without making me feel like anything is missing! I have adored working with you.

Claire, your work on the design and feel of this book has been so beautiful. From the very first version I saw, I knew it was in safe hands. It's like you've taken everything I've loved in cookbooks my whole life and distilled them into a work of my very own. And that feels so special.

Everyone that worked with me to bring the recipes to life with the photography – Ola, Martyna, Sam, Anna, Allegra, and Lu – you should know how mindboggling it was to be in a room with so many incredibly talented people. I learnt so much from you all and it was amazing to see my book take shape through your work.

To my PhD supervisor, Sue: I wouldn't be able to juggle these projects without your patience and support, and I'm so grateful. I know I promised at the end of my first book that I wouldn't write any more books until I finished my PhD, and did not stick to that, so I'm sorry! What can I say – things snowballed. I make no such promises this time but really hope that I'll be finished with my PhD by the time this book hits shelves!

Finally, to the gluten-free community that have rallied behind me over the last few years, none of this would be possible without you. It's through your enthusiasm and encouragement that I continue to find joy in creating recipes. It's also thanks to your support of my first book that this one has been made possible. I hope you love it just as much. And please, never feel strange about sending me photos of your creations on socials – I don't think I'll ever get tired of seeing you make and enjoy my recipes.

*Thank you all!*

# ABOUT THE AUTHOR

**Melanie Persson** (aka **The Very Hungry Coeliac**) was on MasterChef Australia 2022 and was the first contestant to compete as a gluten-free cook. Since being diagnosed with coeliac disease in 2016, she has worked hard to develop recipes that she used to love, sharing them with the community she's built on Instagram. These are strongly influenced by her experiences living in the UK, Australia, Japan and Italy, as well as her Swedish heritage. Mel is passionate about helping people on gluten-free diets rediscover their joy for food and cooking. Whenever she isn't cooking and sharing recipes, she is working on her research as a PhD candidate in the field of children's literature. Her first book, *The Very Hungry Coeliac*, was published in 2023.

Published in 2025 by Hardie Grant Books, an imprint of Hardie Grant Publishing

Hardie Grant Books (Melbourne)
Wurundjeri Country
Level 11, 36 Wellington Street
Collingwood, Victoria 3066

Hardie Grant North America
2912 Telegraph Ave
Berkeley, California 94705

hardiegrant.com/books

Hardie Grant acknowledges the Traditional Owners of the Country on which we work, the Wurundjeri People of the Kulin Nation and the Gadigal People of the Eora Nation, and recognises their continuing connection to the land, waters and culture. We pay our respects to their Elders past and present.

All rights reserved. No part of this publication may be reproduced, stored in a retrieval system or transmitted in any form by any means, electronic, mechanical, photocopying, recording or otherwise, without the prior written permission of the publishers and copyright holders.

The moral rights of the author have been asserted.

Copyright text © Melanie Persson 2025
Copyright photography © Ola Smit 2025
Copyright design © Hardie Grant Publishing 2025

 A catalogue record for this book is available from the National Library of Australia

Gluten-free Feasts

ISBN 978 1 76145 070 9
ISBN 978 1 76145 071 6 (ebook)

10 9 8 7 6 5 4 3 2 1

**Publisher:** Simon Davis
**Head of Editorial:** Jasmin Chua
**Project Editor:** Harriet Webster
**Editor:** Harriet Webster
**Creative Director:** Kristin Thomas
**Designer:** Claire Rochford
**Photographer:** Ola O. Smit
**Photography Assistant:** Martyna Wlodarska
**Food Stylist:** Sam Dixon
**Food Stylist Assistants:** Allegra D'agostini and Lucy Cottle
**Prop Stylist:** Anna Wilkins
**Head of Production:** Todd Rechner
**Production Controller:** Jessica Harvie

Colour reproduction by Splitting Image Colour Studio.

Printed in China by Leo Paper Products LTD.

The paper this book is printed on is from FSC®-certified forests and other sources. FSC® promotes environmentally responsible, socially beneficial and economically viable management of the world's forests.